THE EMPEROR JONES
ANNA CHRISTIE
THE HAIRY APE

# EUGENE O'NEILL

# THE EMPEROR JONES
# ANNA CHRISTIE
# THE HAIRY APE

**VINTAGE BOOKS**

*A Division of Random House*     *New York*

VINTAGE BOOKS EDITION, NOVEMBER 1972

*The Emperor Jones*
COPYRIGHT, 1921 BY HORACE LIVERIGHT, INC.
COPYRIGHT RENEWED, 1948, BY EUGENE O'NEILL

*Anna Christie*
COPYRIGHT, 1922, BY HORACE LIVERIGHT, INC.
COPYRIGHT RENEWED, 1949, BY EUGENE O'NEILL

*The Hairy Ape*
COPYRIGHT, 1922, BY HORACE LIVERIGHT, INC.
COPYRIGHT RENEWED, 1949, BY EUGENE O'NEILL

All rights reserved under International and Pan-American Copyright Conventions. Published in the United States by Random House, Inc., New York. Distributed in Canada by Random House of Canada Limited, Toronto. The Three Plays were originally published by Horace Liveright, Inc., as follows: *The Emperor Jones* in 1921, *Anna Christie* in 1922, *The Hairy Ape* in 1922. The plays were in a collection by *The Modern Library* in 1937. CAUTION: Professionals and amateurs are hereby warned that these plays, being fully protected under the Copyright Laws of the United States of America, the British Commonwealth, including the Dominion of Canada, and all other countries of the Berne and Universal Copyright Conventions, are subject to royalty. All rights, including professional, amateur, recording, motion picture, recitation, lecturing, public reading, radio and television broadcasting, and the rights of translation into foreign languages, are strictly reserved.

Particular emphasis is laid on the question of readings. Inquiries regarding amateur performance rights to these plays should be addressed to Dramatists Play Service, Inc., 440 Park Avenue South, New York, N.Y. 10016. Inquiries regarding stock rights should be addressed to Samuel French, Inc., 25 West 45th Street, New York, N.Y. 10036. All other inquiries should be directed to Cadwalader, Wickersham and Taft, 1 Wall Street, New York, N.Y. 10005.

Library of Congress Cataloging in Publication Data

O'Neill, Eugene Gladstone, 1888–1953.
The Emperor Jones.

Original ed. issued in series: The Modern library of the world's best books.

I. O'Neill, Eugene Gladstone, 1888–1953. Anna Christie. 1972. II. O'Neill, Eugene Gladstone, 1888–1953. The hairy ape. 1972. III. Title. IV. Title: Anna Christie. V. Title: The hairy ape. [PS3529.N5A6 1972b] 812'.5'2 72-4211
ISBN 0-394-71855-0

*Manufactured in the United States of America*

# CONTENTS

The Emperor Jones    1

Anna Christie    55

The Hairy Ape    161

# THE EMPEROR JONES

# THE EMPEROR JONES

## SCENE ONE

SCENE *The audience chamber in the palace of the Emperor—a spacious, high-ceilinged room with bare, white-washed walls. The floor is of white tiles. In the rear, to the left of center, a wide archway giving out on a portico with white pillars. The palace is evidently situated on high ground, for beyond the portico nothing can be seen but a vista of distant hills, their summits crowned with thick groves of palm trees. In the right wall, center, a smaller arched doorway leading to the living quarters of the palace. The room is bare of furniture with the exception of one huge chair made of uncut wood which stands at center, its back to rear. This is very apparently the Emperor's throne. It is painted a dazzling, eye-smiting scarlet. There is a brilliant orange cushion on the seat and another smaller one is placed on the floor to serve as a footstool. Strips of matting, dyed scarlet, lead from the foot of the throne to the two entrances.*

*It is late afternoon but the sunlight still*

*blazes yellowly beyond the portico and there is an oppressive burden of exhausting heat in the air.*

*As the curtain rises, a native Negro woman sneaks in cautiously from the entrance on the right. She is very old, dressed in cheap calico, bare-footed, a red bandana handkerchief covering all but a few stray wisps of white hair. A bundle bound in colored cloth is carried over her shoulder on the end of a stick. She hesitates beside the doorway, peering back as if in extreme dread of being discovered. Then she begins to glide noiselessly a step at a time, toward the doorway in the rear. At this moment,* SMITHERS *appears beneath the portico.*

SMITHERS *is a tall, stoop-shouldered man about forty. His bald head, perched on a long neck with an enormous Adam's apple, looks like an egg. The tropics have tanned his naturally pasty face with its small, sharp features to a sickly yellow, and native rum has painted his pointed nose to a startling red. His little, washy-blue eyes are red-rimmed and dart about him like a ferret's. His expression is one of unscrupulous meanness, cowardly and dangerous. He is dressed in a worn riding suit of dirty white drill, puttees, spurs, and wears a white cork helmet. A cartridge belt with an automatic revolver is around his waist. He carries a riding whip in his hand.*

# CHARACTERS

BRUTUS JONES, *Emperor*
HENRY SMITHERS, *A Cockney Trader*
AN OLD NATIVE WOMAN
LEM, *A Native Chief*
SOLDIERS, *Adherents of Lem*
The Little Formless Fears; Jeff; The Negro Convicts; The Prison Guard; The Planters; The Auctioneer; The Slaves; The Congo Witch-Doctor; The Crocodile God

*The action of the play takes place on an island in the West Indies as yet not self-determined by white Marines. The form of native government is, for the time being, an empire.*

*He sees the woman and stops to watch her suspiciously. Then, making up his mind, he steps quickly on tiptoe into the room. The woman, looking back over her shoulder continually, does not see him until it is too late. When she does* SMITHERS *springs forward and grabs her firmly by the shoulder. She struggles to get away, fiercely but silently.*

SMITHERS [*Tightening his grasp—roughly*] Easy! None o' that, me birdie. You can't wriggle out now. I got me 'ooks on yer.

WOMAN [*Seeing the uselessness of struggling, gives way to frantic terror, and sinks to the ground, embracing his knees supplicatingly*] No tell him! No tell him, Mister!

SMITHERS [*With great curiosity*] Tell 'im? [*Then scornfully.*] Oh, you mean 'is bloomin' Majesty. What's the gaime, any 'ow? What are you sneakin' away for? Been stealin' a bit, I s'pose. [*He taps her bundle with his riding whip significantly.*]

WOMAN [*Shaking her head vehemently*] No, me no steal.

SMITHERS Bloody liar! But tell me what's up. There's somethin' funny goin' on. I smelled it in the air first thing I got up this mornin'. You blacks are up to some devilment. This palace of 'is is like a bleedin' tomb. Where's all the 'ands? [*The woman keeps sullenly silent.* SMITHERS *raises his whip threateningly.*] Ow, yer won't, won't yer? I'll show yer what's what.

WOMAN [*Coweringly*] I tell, Mister. You no hit. They go—all go. [*She makes a sweeping gesture toward the hills in the distance.*]

SMITHERS  Run away—to the 'ills?

WOMAN  Yes, Mister. Him Emperor—Great Father. [*She touches her forehead to the floor with a quick mechanical jerk.*] Him sleep after eat. Then they go—all go. Me old woman. Me left only. Now me go too.

SMITHERS [*His astonishment giving way to an immense, mean satisfaction*] Ow! So that's the ticket! Well, I know bloody well wot's in the air—when they runs orf to the 'ills. The tom-tom 'll be thumping out there bloomin' soon. [*With extreme vindictiveness.*] And I'm bloody glad of it, for one! Serve 'im right! Puttin' on airs, the stinkin' nigger! 'Is Majesty! Gawd blimey! I only 'opes I'm there when they takes 'im out to shoot 'im. [*Suddenly*] 'E's still 'ere all right, ain't 'e?

WOMAN  Yes. Him sleep.

SMITHERS  'E's bound to find out soon as 'e wakes up. 'E's cunnin' enough to know when 'is time's come. [*He goes to the doorway on right and whistles shrilly with his fingers in his mouth. The old woman springs to her feet and runs out of the doorway, rear. SMITHERS goes after her, reaching for his revolver.*] Stop or I'll shoot! [*Then stopping—indifferently*] Pop orf then, if yer like, yer black cow. [*He stands in the doorway, looking after her.*]

[JONES *enters from the right. He is a tall, powerfully-built, full-blooded Negro of middle age. His features are typically negroid, yet there is something decidedly distinctive about his face—an underlying strength of will, a hardy, self-reliant confidence in himself that inspires respect. His eyes are alive with a keen, cunning intelligence. In manner he is shrewd, suspicious, evasive. He wears a light blue uniform coat, sprayed with brass buttons, heavy gold chevrons on his shoulders, gold braid on the collar, cuffs, etc. His pants are bright red with a light blue stripe down the side. Patent-leather laced boots with brass spurs, and a belt with a long-barreled, pearl-handled revolver in a holster complete his make up. Yet there is something not altogether ridiculous about his grandeur. He has a way of carrying it off.*]

JONES [*Not seeing anyone—greatly irritated and blinking sleepily—shouts*] Who dare whistle dat way in my palace? Who dare wake up de Emperor? I'll git de hide fravled off some o' you niggers sho'!

SMITHERS [*Showing himself—in a manner half-afraid and half-defiant*] It was me whistled to yer. [*As* JONES *frowns angrily*] I got news for yer.

JONES [*Putting on his suavest manner, which fails to cover up his contempt for the white man*] Oh, it's you, Mister Smithers. [*He sits down on his throne with easy dignity.*] What news you got to tell me?

SMITHERS [*Coming close to enjoy his discomfiture*] Don't yer notice nothin' funny today?

JONES [*Coldly*] Funny? No, I ain't perceived nothin' of de kind!

SMITHERS Then yer ain't so foxy as I thought yer

was. Where's all your court? [*Sarcastically*] The Generals and the Cabinet Ministers and all?

JONES [*Imperturbably*] Where dey mostly runs de minute I close my eyes—drinkin' rum and talkin' big down in de town. [*Sarcastically*] How come you don't know dat? Ain't you sousin' with 'em most every day?

SMITHERS [*Stung but pretending indifference—with a wink*] That's part of the day's work. I got ter—ain't I—in my business?

JONES [*Contemptuously*] Yo' business!

SMITHERS [*Imprudently enraged*] Gawd blimey, you was glad enough for me ter take yer in on it when you landed here first. You didn' 'ave no 'igh and mighty airs in them days!

JONES [*His hand going to his revolver like a flash—menacingly*] Talk polite, white man! Talk polite, you heah me! I'm boss heah now, is you fergettin'? [*The Cockney seems about to challenge this last statement with the facts but something in the other's eyes holds and cows him.*]

SMITHERS [*In a cowardly whine*] No 'arm meant, old top.

JONES [*Condescendingly*] I accept yo' apology. [*Lets his hand fall from his revolver.*] No use'n you rakin' up ole times. What I was den is one thing. What I is now 's another. You didn't let me in on yo' crooked work out o' no kind feelin's dat time. I done de dirty work fo' you—and most o' de brain work, too, fo' dat matter—and I was wu'th money to you, dat's de reason.

SMITHERS  Well, blimey, I give yer a start, didn't I—when no one else would. I wasn't afraid to 'ire yer like the rest was—'count of the story about your breakin' jail back in the States.

JONES  No, you didn't have no s'cuse to look down on me fo' dat. You been in jail you'self more'n once.

SMITHERS [*Furiously*]  It's a lie! [*Then trying to pass it off by an attempt at scorn*] Garn! Who told yer that fairy tale?

JONES  Dey's some tings I ain't got to be tole. I kin see 'em in folk's eyes. [*Then after a pause—meditatively*] Yes, you sho' give me a start. And it didn't take long from dat time to git dese fool, woods' niggers right where I wanted dem. [*With pride*] From stowaway to Emperor in two years! Dat's goin' some!

SMITHERS [*With curiosity*]  And I bet you got yer pile o' money 'id safe some place.

JONES [*With satisfaction*]  I sho' has! And it's in a foreign bank where no pusson don't ever git it out but me no matter what come. You didn't s'pose I was holdin' down dis Emperor job for de glory in it, did you? Sho'! De fuss and glory part of it, dat's only to turn de heads o' de low-flung, bush niggers dat's here. Dey wants de big circus show for deir money. I gives it to 'em an' I gits de money. [*With a grin*] De long green, dat's me every time! [*Then rebukingly*] But you ain't got no kick agin me, Smithers. I'se paid you back all you done for me many times. Ain't I pertected you and winked at all de crooked tradin' you been doin' right out in de broad day?

Sho' I has—and me makin' laws to stop it at de same time! [*He chuckles.*]

SMITHERS [*Grinning*] But, meanin' no 'arm, you been grabbin' right and left yourself, ain't yer? Look at the taxes you've put on 'em! Blimey! You've squeezed 'em dry!

JONES [*Chuckling*] No, dey ain't *all* dry yet. I'se still heah, ain't I?

SMITHERS [*Smiling at his secret thought*] They're dry right now, you'll find out. [*Changing the subject abruptly.*] And as for me breakin' laws, you've broke 'em all yerself just as fast as yer made 'em.

JONES Ain't I de Emperor? De laws don't go for him. [*Judicially*] You heah what I tells you, Smithers. Dere's little stealin' like you does, and dere's big stealin' like I does. For de little stealin' dey gits you in jail soon or late. For de big stealin' dey makes you Emperor and puts you in de Hall o' Fame when you croaks. [*Reminiscently*] If dey's one thing I learns in ten years on de Pullman ca's listenin' to de white quality talk, it's dat same fact. And when I gits a chance to use it I winds up Emperor in two years.

SMITHERS [*Unable to repress the genuine admiration of the small fry for the large*] Yes, yer turned the bleedin' trick, all right. Blimey, I never seen a bloke 'as 'ad the bloomin' luck you 'as.

JONES [*Severely*] Luck? What you mean—luck?

SMITHERS I suppose you'll say as that swank about the silver bullet ain't luck—and that was what first got the fool blacks on yer side the time of the revolution, wasn't it?

JONES [*With a laugh*] Oh, dat silver bullet! Sho' was luck! But I makes dat luck, you heah? I loads de dice! Yessuh! When dat murderin' nigger ole Lem hired to kill me takes aim ten feet away and his gun misses fire and I shoots him dead, what you heah me say?

SMITHERS You said yer'd got a charm so's no lead bullet'd kill yer. You was so strong only a silver bullet could kill yer, you told 'em. Blimey, wasn't that swank for yer—and plain, fat-'eaded luck?

JONES [*Proudly*] I got brains and I uses 'em quick. Dat ain't luck.

SMITHERS Yer know they wasn't 'ardly liable to get no silver bullets. And it was luck 'e didn't 'it you that time.

JONES [*Laughing*] And dere all dem fool, bush niggers was kneelin' down and bumpin' deir heads on de ground like I was a miracle out o' de Bible. Oh Lawd, from dat time on I had dem all eatin' out of my hand. I cracks de whip and dey jumps through.

SMITHERS [*With a sniff*] Yankee bluff done it.

JONES Ain't a man's talkin' big what makes him big—long as he makes folks believe it? Sho', I talks large when I ain't got nothin' to back it up, but I ain't talkin' wild just de same. I knows I kin fool 'em—I *knows* it—and dat's backin' enough fo' my game. And ain't I got to learn deir lingo and teach some of dem English befo' I kin to talk to 'em? Ain't dat wuk? You ain't never learned ary word er it, Smithers, in de ten years you been heah, dough yo' knows it's money in yo' pocket tradin' wid 'em if you does. But you'se too shiftless to take de trouble.

SMITHERS [*Flushing*] Never mind about me. What's this I've 'eard about yer really 'avin' a silver bullet moulded for yourself?

JONES It's playin' out my bluff. I has de silver bullet moulded and I tells 'em when de time comes I kills myself wid it. I tells 'em dat's 'cause I'm de on'y man in de world big enough to git me. No use'n deir tryin'. And dey falls down and bumps deir heads. [*He laughs.*] I does dat so's I kin take a walk in peace widout no jealous nigger gunnin' at me from behind de trees.

SMITHERS [*Astonished*] Then you 'ad it made—'onest?

JONES Sho' did. Heah she be. [*He takes out his revolver, breaks it, and takes the silver bullet out of one chamber.*] Five lead an' dis silver baby at de last. Don't she shine pretty? [*He holds it in his hand, looking at it admiringly, as if strangely fascinated.*]

SMITHERS Let me see. [*Reaches out his hand for it.*]

JONES [*Harshly*] Keep yo' hands whar dey b'long, white man. [*He replaces it in the chamber and puts the revolver back on his hip.*]

SMITHERS [*Snarling*] Gawd blimey! Think I'm a bleedin' thief, you would.

JONES No, 'tain't dat. I knows you'se scared to steal from me. On'y I ain't 'lowin' nary body to touch dis baby. She's my rabbit's foot.

SMITHERS [*Sneering*] A bloomin' charm, wot?

[*Venomously*] Well, you'll need all the bloody charms you 'as before long, s' 'elp me!

JONES [*Judicially*]   Oh, I'se good for six months yit 'fore dey gits sick o' my game. Den, when I sees trouble comin', I makes my getaway.

SMITHERS   Ho! You got it all planned, ain't yer?

JONES   I ain't no fool. I knows dis Emperor's time is sho't. Dat why I make hay when de sun shine. Was you thinkin' I'se aimin' to hold down dis job for life? No, suh! What good is gittin' money if you stays back in dis raggedy country? I wants action when I spends. And when I sees dese niggers gittin' up deir nerve to tu'n me out, and I'se got all de money in sight, I resigns on de spot and beats it quick.

SMITHERS   Where to?

JONES   None o' yo' business.

SMITHERS   Not back to the bloody States, I'll lay my oath.

JONES [*Suspiciously*]   Why don't I? [*Then with an easy laugh*] You mean 'count of dat story 'bout me breakin' from jail back dere? Dat's all talk.

SMITHERS [*Skeptically*]   Ho, yes!

JONES [*Sharply*]   You ain't 'sinuatin' I'se a liar, is you?

SMITHERS [*Hastily*]   No, Gawd strike me! I was only thinkin' o' the bloody lies you told the blacks 'ere about killin' white men in the States.

JONES [*Angered*]   How come dey're lies?

SMITHERS   You'd 'ave been in jail if you 'ad, wouldn't yer then? [*With venom*] And from what

I've 'eard, it ain't 'ealthy for a black to kill a white man in the States. They burns 'em in oil, don't they?

JONES [*With cool deadliness*] You mean lynchin' 'd scare me? Well, I tells you, Smithers, maybe I does kill one white man back dere. Maybe I does. And maybe I kills another right heah 'fore long if he don't look out.

SMITHERS [*Trying to force a laugh*] I was on'y spoofin' yer. Can't yer take a joke? And you was just sayin' you'd never been in jail.

JONES [*In the same tone—slightly boastful*] Maybe I goes to jail dere for gettin' in an argument wid razors ovah a crap game. Maybe I gits twenty years when dat colored man die. Maybe I gits in 'nother argument wid de prison guard was overseer ovah us when we're wukin' de roads. Maybe he hits me wid a whip and I splits his head wid a shovel and runs away and files de chain off my leg and gits away safe. Maybe I does all dat an' maybe I don't. It's a story I tells you so's you knows I'se de kind of man dat if you evah repeats one word of it, I ends yo' stealin' on dis yearth mighty damn quick!

SMITHERS [*Terrified*] Think I'd peach on yer? Not me! Ain't I always been yer friend?

JONES [*Suddenly relaxing*] Sho' you has—and you better be.

SMITHERS [*Recovering his composure—and with it his malice*] And just to show yer I'm yer friend, I'll tell yer that bit o' news I was goin' to.

JONES Go ahead! Shoot de piece. Must be bad news from de happy way you look.

SMITHERS [*Warningly*] Maybe it's gettin' time for you to resign—with that bloomin' silver bullet, wot? [*He finishes with a mocking grin.*]

JONES [*Puzzled*] What's dat you say? Talk plain.

SMITHERS Ain't noticed any of the guards or servants about the place today, I 'aven't.

JONES [*Carelessly*] Dey're all out in de garden sleepin' under de trees. When I sleeps, dey sneaks a sleep, too, and I pretends I never suspicions it. All I got to do is to ring de bell and dey come flyin', makin' a bluff dey was wukin' all de time.

SMITHERS [*In the same mocking tone*] Ring the bell now an' you'll bloody well see what I means.

JONES [*Startled to alertness, but preserving the same careless tone*] Sho' I rings. [*He reaches below the throne and pulls out a big, common dinner bell which is painted the same vivid scarlet as the throne. He rings this vigorously—then stops to listen. Then he goes to both doors, rings again, and looks out.*]

SMITHERS [*Watching him with malicious satisfaction, after a pause—mockingly*] The bloody ship is sinkin' an' the bleedin' rats 'as slung their 'ooks.

JONES [*In a sudden fit of anger flings the bell clattering into a corner*] Low-flung, woods' niggers! [*Then catching Smithers' eye on him, he controls himself and suddenly bursts into a low chuckling laugh.*] Reckon I overplays my hand dis once! A man can't take de pot on a bob-tailed flush all de time. Was I sayin' I'd sit in six months mo'? Well, I'se changed my mind den, I cashes in and resigns de job of Emperor right dis minute.

SMITHERS [*With real admiration*] Blimey, but you're a cool bird, and no mistake.

JONES  No use'n fussin'. When I knows de game's up I kisses it good-bye widout no long waits. Dey've all run off to de hills, ain't dey?

SMITHERS  Yes—every bleedin' man jack of 'em.

JONES  Den de revolution is at de post. And de Emperor better git his feet smokin' up de trail. [*He starts for the door in rear.*]

SMITHERS  Goin' out to look for your 'orse? Yer won't find any. They steals the 'orses first thing. Mine was gone when I went for 'im this mornin'. That's wot first give me a suspicion of wot was up.

JONES [*Alarmed for a second, scratches his head, then philosophically*]  Well, den I hoofs it. Feet, do yo' duty! [*He pulls out a gold watch and looks at it.*] Three-thuty. Sundown's at six-thuty or dereabouts. [*Puts his watch back—with cool confidence.*] I got plenty o' time to make it easy.

SMITHERS  Don't be so bloomin' sure of it. They'll be after you 'ot and 'eavy. Ole Lem is at the bottom o' this business an' 'e 'ates you like 'ell. 'E'd rather do for you than eat 'is dinner, 'e would!

JONES [*Scornfully*]  Dat fool no-count nigger! Does you think I'se scared o' him? I stands him on his thick head mor'n once befo' dis, and I does it again if he come in my way . . . [*Fiercely*] And dis time I leave him a dead nigger fo' sho'!

SMITHERS  You'll 'ave to cut through the big forest—an' these blacks 'ere can sniff and follow a trail in the dark like 'ounds. You'd 'ave to 'ustle to get through that forest in twelve hours even if you knew all the bloomin' trails like a native.

JONES [*With indignant scorn*] Look-a-heah, white man! Does you think I'se a natural bo'n fool? Give me credit fo' havin' some sense, fo' Lawd's sake! Don't you s'pose I'se looked ahead and made sho' of all de chances? I'se gone out in dat big forest, pretendin' to hunt, so many times dat I knows it high an' low like a book. I could go through on dem trails wid my eyes shut. [*With great contempt*] Think dese ign'rent bush niggers dat ain't got brains enuff to know deir own names even can catch Brutus Jones? Huh, I s'pects not! Not on yo' life! Why, man, de white men went after me wid bloodhounds where I come from an I jes' laughs at 'em. It's a shame to fool dese black trash around heah, dey're so easy. You watch me, man! I'll make dem look sick, I will. I'll be 'cross de plain to de edge of de forest by time dark comes. Once in de woods in de night, dey got a swell chance o' findin' dis baby! Dawn tomorrow I'll be out at de oder side and on de coast whar dat French gunboat is stayin'. She picks me up, take me to Martinique when she go dar, and dere I is safe wid a mighty big bankroll in my jeans. It's easy as rollin' off a log.

SMITHERS [*Maliciously*] But s'posin' somethin' 'appens wrong an' they do nab yer?

JONES [*Decisively*] Dey don't—dat's de answer.

SMITHERS But, just for argyment's sake—what'd you do?

JONES [*Frowning*] I'se got five lead bullets in dis

gun good enuff fo' common bush niggers—and after dat I got de silver bullet left to cheat 'em out o' gittin' me.

SMITHERS [*Jeeringly*] Ho, I was fergettin' that silver bullet. You'll bump yourself orf in style, won't yer? Blimey!

JONES [*Gloomily*] You kin bet yo whole roll on one thing, white man. Dis baby plays out his string to de end and when he quits, he quits wid a bang de way he ought. Silver bullet ain't none too good for him when he go, dat's a fac'! [*Then shaking off his nervousness—with a confident laugh*] Sho'! What is I talkin' about? Ain't come to dat yit and I never will—not wid trash niggers like dese yere. [*Boastfully*] Silver bullet bring me luck anyway. I kin outguess, outrun, outfight, an' outplay de whole lot o' dem all ovah de board any time o' de day er night! You watch me! [*From the distant hills comes the faint, steady thump of a tom-tom, low and vibrating. It starts at a rate exactly corresponding to normal pulse beat—72 to the minute—and continues at a gradually accelerating rate from this point uninterruptedly to the very end of the play.*]

[JONES *starts at the sound. A strange look of apprehension creeps into his face for a moment as he listens. Then he asks, with an attempt to regain his most casual manner*] What's dat drum beatin' fo'?

SMITHERS [*With a mean grin*] For you. That means the bleedin' ceremony 'as started. I've 'eard it before and I knows.

JONES Cer'mony? What cer'mony?

SMITHERS  The blacks is 'oldin' a bloody meetin', 'avin' a war dance, gettin' their courage worked up b'fore they starts after you.

JONES  Let dem! Dey'll sho' need it!

SMITHERS  And they're there 'oldin their 'eathen religious service—makin' no end of devil spells and charms to 'elp 'em against your silver bullet. [*He guffaws loudly.*] Blimey, but they're balmy as 'ell!

JONES [*A tiny bit awed and shaken in spite of himself*] Huh! Takes more'n dat to scare dis chicken!

SMITHERS [*Scenting the other's feeling—maliciously*]  Ternight when it's pitch black in the forest, they'll 'ave their pet devils and ghosts 'oundin' after you. You'll find yer bloody 'air 'll be standin' on end before termorrow mornin'. [*Seriously*] It's a bleedin' queer place, that stinkin' forest, even in daylight. Yer don't know what might 'appen in there, it's that rotten still. Always sends the cold shivers down my back minute I gets in it.

JONES [*With a contemptuous sniff*] I ain't no chicken-liver like you is. Trees an' me, we'se friends, and dar's a full moon comin' bring me light. And let dem po' niggers make all de fool spells dey'se a min' to. Does yo' s'pect I'se silly enuff to b'lieve in ghosts an' ha'ants an' all dat ole woman's talk? G'long, white man! You ain't talkin' to me. [*With a chuckle*] Doesn't you know dey's got to do wid a man was member in good standin' o' de Baptist Church? Sho' I was dat when I was porter on de Pullmans, befo' I gits into my little trouble. Let dem try deir heathen tricks. De Baptist Church done pertect me and land dem all in hell. [*Then with more confident satisfaction*] And I'se got little silver bullet o' my own, don't forgit.

SMITHERS Ho! You 'aven't give much 'eed to your Baptist Church since you been down 'ere. I've 'eard myself you 'ad turned yer coat an' was takin' up with their blarsted witch-doctors, or whatever the 'ell yer calls the swine.

JONES [*Vehemently*] I pretends to! Sho' I pretends! Dat's part o' my game from de fust. If I finds out dem niggers believes dat black is white, den I yells it out louder 'n deir loudest. It don't git me nothin' to do missionary work for de Baptist Church. I'se after de coin, an' I lays my Jesus on de shelf for de time bein'. [*Stops abruptly to look at his watch—alertly.*] But I ain't got de time to waste no more fool talk wid you. I'se gwine away from heah dis secon'. [*He reaches in under the throne and pulls out an expensive Panama hat with a bright multi-colored band and sets it jauntily on his head.*] So long, white man! [*With a grin*] See you in jail sometime, maybe!

SMITHERS Not me, you won't. Well, I wouldn't be in your bloody boots for no bloomin' money, but 'ere's wishin' yer luck just the same.

JONES [*Contemptuously*] You're de frightenedest man evah I see! I tells you I'se safe's 'f I was in New York City. It takes dem niggers from now to dark to git up de nerve to start somethin'. By dat time, I'se got a head start dey never kotch up wid.

SMITHERS [*Maliciously*] Give my regards to any ghosts yer meets up with.

JONES [*Grinning*] If dat ghost got money, I'll tell him never ha'nt you less'n he wants to lose it.

SMITHERS [*Flattered*] Garn! [*Then curiously*] Ain't yer takin' no luggage with yer?

JONES  I travels light when I want to move fast. And I got tinned grub buried on de edge o' de forest. [*Boastfully*] Now say that I don't look ahead an' use my brains! [*With a wide, liberal gesture*] I will all dat's left in de palace to you—and you better grab all you kin sneak away wid befo' dey gits here.

SMITHERS [*Gratefully*] Righto—and thanks ter yer. [*As* JONES *walks toward the door in rear—cautioningly*] Say! Look 'ere, you ain't goin' out that way, are yer?

JONES  Does you think I'd slink out de back door like a common nigger? I'se Emperor yit, ain't I? And de Emperor Jones leaves de way he comes, and dat black trash don't dare stop him—not yit, leastways. [*He stops for a moment in the doorway, listening to the far-off but insistent beat of the tom-tom.*] Listen to dat roll-call, will you? Must be mighty big drum carry dat far. [*Then with a laugh*] Well, if dey ain't no whole brass band to see me off, I sho' got de drum part of it. So long, white man. [*He puts his hands in his pockets and with studied carelessness, whistling a tune, he saunters out of the doorway and off to the left.*]

SMITHERS [*Looks after him with a puzzled admiration*] 'E's got 'ise bloomin' nerve with 'im, s'elp me! [*Then angrily*] Ho—the bleedin' nigger—puttin' on 'is bloody airs! I 'opes they nabs 'im an' gives 'im what's what! [*Then putting business before the pleasure of this thought, looking around him with cupidity*] A bloke ought to find a 'ole lot in this palace that'd go for a bit of cash. Let's take a look, 'Arry, me lad. [*He starts for the doorway on right as*

[*The curtain falls.*]

# SCENE TWO

SCENE *Nightfall. The end of the plain where the Great Forest begins. The foreground is sandy, level ground dotted by a few stones and clumps of stunted bushes cowering close against the earth to escape the buffeting of the trade wind. In the rear the forest is a wall of darkness dividing the world. Only when the eye becomes accustomed to the gloom can the outlines of separate trunks of the nearest trees be made out, enormous pillars of deeper blackness. A somber monotone of wind lost in the leaves moans in the air. Yet this sound serves but to intensify the impression of the forest's relentless immobility, to form a background throwing into relief its brooding, implacable silence.*

[JONES *enters from the left, walking rapidly. He stops as he nears the edge of the forest, looks around him quickly, peering into the dark as if searching for some familiar landmark. Then, apparently satisfied that he is where he ought to be, he throws himself on the ground, dog-tired.*]

Well, heah I is. In de nick o' time, too! Little mo' an' it'd be blacker'n de ace of spades heah-abouts. [*He pulls a bandana handkerchief from his hip pocket and mops off his perspiring face.*] Sho'! Gimme air! I'se tuckered out sho' nuff. Dat soft Emperor job ain't no trainin' fo' a long hike ovah dat plain in de brilin' sun. [*Then with a chuckle*] Cheah up, nigger, de worst is yet to come. [*He lifts his head and stares at the forest. His chuckle peters out abruptly. In a tone of awe*] My goodness, look at dem woods, will you? Dat no-count Smithers said dey'd be black an' he sho' called de turn. [*Turning away from them quickly and looking down at his feet, he snatches at a chance to change the subject —solicitously*] Feet, you is holdin' up yo' end fine an' I sutinly hopes you ain't blisterin' none. It's time you git a rest. [*He takes off his shoes, his eyes studiously avoiding the forest. He feels of the soles of his feet gingerly.*] You is still in de pink—on'y a little mite feverish. Cool yo'selfs. Remember you done got a long journey yit befo' you. [*He sits in a weary attitude, listening to the rhythmic beating of the tom-tom. He grumbles in a loud tone to cover up a growing uneasiness.*] Bush niggers! Wonder dey wouldn' git sick o' beatin' dat drum. Sound louder, seem like. I wonder if dey's startin' after me? [*He scrambles to his feet, looking back across the plain.*] Couldn't see dem now, nohow, if dey was hundred feet away. [*Then shaking himself like a wet dog to get rid of these depressing thoughts*] Sho', dey's miles an' miles behind. What you gittin' fidgety about? [*But he sits down and begins to lace up his shoes in great haste, all the time muttering reassuringly.*] You know what? Yo' belly is empty, dat's what's de matter wid you. Come time to eat! Wid nothin' but wind on yo' stumach, o' course you feels jiggedy. Well, we eats right heah an' now soon's I gits dese pesky shoes laced up! [*He finishes lacing up his shoes.*] Dere! Now le's see. [*Gets on his hands and knees and searches the ground around him with his eyes.*] White stone, white stone, where is you? [*He sees the first white stone and crawls to it—with satisfaction.*] Heah you is! I knowed dis was de right place. Box of grub, come to me. [*He turns over the stone and feels under it—in a tone of dismay.*] Ain't heah! Gorry, is I in de right place or isn't I? Dere's 'nother stone. Guess dat's it. [*He scrambles to the next stone and turns it over.*] Ain't heah, neither! Grub, whar is you? Ain't heah. Gorry, has I got to go hungry into dem woods—all de night? [*While he is talking he scrambles from one stone to another, turning them over in frantic haste. Finally, he jumps to his feet excitedly.*] Is I lost de place? Must have! But how dat happen when I was followin' de trail across de plain in broad daylight? [*Almost plaintively*] I'se hungry, I is! I gotta git my feed. Whar's my strength gonna come from if I doesn't? Gorry, I gotta find dat grub high an' low somehow! Why it come dark so quick like dat? Can't see nothin'. [*He scratches a match on his trousers and peers about him. The rate of the beat of the far-off tom-tom in-*

*creases perceptibly as he does so. He mutters in a bewildered voice.*] How come all dese white stones come heah when I only remembers one? [*Suddenly, with a frightened grasp, he flings the match on the ground and stamps on it.*] Nigger, is you gone crazy mad? Is you lightin' matches to show dem whar you is? Fo' Lawd's sake, use yo' haid. Gorry, I'se got to be careful! [*He stares at the plain behind him apprehensively, his hand on his revolver.*] But how come all dese white stones? And whar's dat tin box o' grub I had all wrapped up in oil cloth?

[*While his back is turned, the* LITTLE FORMLESS FEARS *creep out from the deeper blackness of the forest. They are black, shapeless, only their glittering little eyes can be seen. If they have any describable form at all it is that of a grubworm about the size of a creeping child. They move noiselessly, but with deliberate, painful effort, striving to raise themselves on end, failing and sinking prone again.* JONES *turns about to face the forest. He stares up at the tops of the trees, seeking vainly to discover his whereabouts by their conformation.*]

Can't tell nothin' from dem trees! Gorry, nothin' 'round heah look like I evah seed it befo'. I'se done lost de place sho' 'nuff! [*With mournful foreboding*] It's mighty queer! It's mighty queer! [*With sudden forced defiance—in an angry tone*] Woods, is you tryin' to put somethin' ovah on me?

[*From the formless creatures on the ground in front of him comes a tiny gale of low mocking laugh-*

*ter like a rustling of leaves. They squirm upward toward him in twisted attitudes.* JONES *looks down, leaps backward with a yell of terror, yanking out his revolver as he does so—in a quavering voice*] What's dat? Who's dar? What is you? Git away from me befo' I shoots you up! You don't? . . .

> [*He fires. There is a flash, a loud report, then silence broken only by the far-off, quickened throb of the tom-tom. The formless creatures have scurried back into the forest.* JONES *remains fixed in his position, listening intently. The sound of the shot, the reassuring feel of the revolver in his hand, have somewhat restored his shaken nerve. He addresses himself with renewed confidence.*]

Dey're gone. Dat shot fix 'em. Dey was only little animals—little wild pigs, I reckon. Dey've maybe rooted out yo' grub an' eat it. Sho', you fool nigger, what you think dey is—ha'nts? [*Excitedly*] Gorry, you give de game away when you fire dat shot. Dem niggers heah dat fo' su'tin! Time you beat in de woods widout no long waits. [*He starts for the forest—hesitates before the plunge—then urging himself in with manful resolution*] Git in, nigger! What you skeered at? Ain't nothin' dere but de trees! Git in! [*He plunges boldly into the forest.*]

# SCENE THREE

SCENE *Nine o'clock. In the forest. The moon has just risen. It beams, drifting through the canopy of leaves, makes a barely perceptible, suffused, eerie glow. A dense low wall of underbrush and creepers is in the nearer foreground, fencing in a small triangular clearing. Beyond this is the massed blackness of the forest like an encompassing barrier. A path is dimly discerned leading down to the clearing from left, rear, and winding away from it again toward the right. As the scene opens nothing can be distinctly made out. Except for the beating of the tom-tom, which is a trifle louder and quicker than in the previous scene, there is silence, broken every few seconds by a queer, clicking sound. Then gradually the figure of the Negro,* JEFF, *can be discerned crouching on his haunches at the rear of the triangle. He is middle-aged, thin, brown in color, is dressed in a Pullman porter's uniform, cap, etc. He is throwing a pair of dice on the ground before him, pick-*

*ing them up, shaking them, casting them out with the regular, rigid, mechanical movements of an automaton. The heavy, plodding footsteps of someone approaching along the trail from the left are heard and* JONES' *voice, pitched in a slightly higher key and strained in a cheering effort to overcome its own tremors.*

De moon's rizen. Does you heah dat, nigger? You gits more light from dis out. No mo' buttin' yo' fool head agin' de trunks an' scratchin' de hide off yo' legs in de bushes. Now you sees whar yo'se gwine. So cheer up! From now on you has a snap. [*He steps just to the rear of the triangular clearing and mops off his face on his sleeve. He has lost his Panama hat. His face is scratched, his brilliant uniform shows several large rents.*] What time's it gittin' to be, I wonder? I dassent light no match to find out. Phoo'. It's wa'm an' dat's a fac'! [*Wearily*] How long I been makin' tracks in dese woods? Must be hours an' hours. Seems like fo'evah! Yit can't be, when de moon's jes' riz. Dis am a long night fo' yo', yo' Majesty! [*With a mournful chuckle*] Majesty! Der ain't much majesty 'bout dis baby now. [*With attempted cheerfulness*] Never min'. It's all part o' de game. Dis night come to an end like everything else. And when you gits dar safe and has dat bankroll in yo' hands you laughs at all dis. [*He starts to whistle but checks himself abruptly.*] What yo' whistlin' for, you po' dope! Want all de worl' to heah you? [*He stops talking to listen.*] Heah dat ole drum! Sho' gits nearer from de sound. Dey're packin'

## 32  THE EMPEROR JONES

it along wid 'em. Time fo' me to move. [*He takes a step forward, then stops—worriedly.*] What's dat odder queer clickety sound I heah? Dere it is! Sound close! Sound like—sound like—Fo' God sake, sound like some nigger was shootin' crap! [*Frightenedly*] I better beat it quick when I gits dem notions. [*He walks quickly into the clear space—then stands transfixed as he sees* JEFF—*in a terrified gasp*] Who dar? Who dat? It dat you, Jeff? [*Starting toward the other, forgetful for a moment of his surroundings and really believing it is a living man that he sees—in a tone of happy relief.*] Jeff! I'se sho' mighty glad to see you! Dey tol' me you done died from dat razor cut I gives you. [*Stopping suddenly, bewilderedly*] But how you come to be heah, nigger? [*He stares fascinatedly at the other who continues his mechanical play with the dice.* JONES' *eyes begin to roll wildly. He stutters.*] Ain't you gwine—look up—can't you speaks to me? Is you—is you—a ha'nt? [*He jerks out his revolver in a frenzy of terrified rage.*] Nigger, I kills you dead once. Has I got to kill you again? You take it den. [*He fires. When the smoke clears away* JEFF *has disappeared.* JONES *stands trembling—then with a certain reassurance*] He's gone, anyway. Ha'nt or no ha'nt, dat shot fix him. [*The beat of the far-off tom-tom is perceptibly louder and more rapid.* JONES *becomes conscious of it—with a start, looking back over his shoulder.*] Dey's gittin' near! Dey's comin' fast! And heah I is shootin' shots to let 'em know jes' whar I is. Oh, Gorry, I'se got to run. [*Forgetting the path he plunges wildly into the underbrush in the rear and disappears in the shadow.*]

## SCENE FOUR

SCENE *Eleven o'clock. In the forest. A wide dirt road runs diagonally from right, front, to left, rear. Rising sheer on both sides the forest walls it in. The moon is now up. Under its light the road glimmers ghastly and unreal. It is as if the forest had stood aside momentarily to let the road pass through and accomplish its veiled purpose. This done, the forest will fold in upon itself again and the road will be no more.* JONES *stumbles in from the forest on the right. His uniform is ragged and torn. He looks about him with numbed surprise when he sees the road, his eyes blinking in the bright moonlight. He flops down exhaustedly and pants heavily for a while. Then with sudden anger*

I'm meltin' wid heat! Runnin' an' runnin' an' runnin'! Damn dis heah coat! Like a strait-jacket! [*He tears off his coat and flings it away from him, revealing himself stripped to the waist.*] Dere! Dat's better! Now I kin breathe! [*Looking down at his feet, the spurs catch his eye.*] And to hell wid dese high-fangled spurs. Dey're what's been a-trippin' me up an' breakin' my neck. [*He unstraps them and flings them away disgustedly.*] Dere! I gits rid o' dem frippety Emperor trappin's an' I travels lighter. Lawd! I'se tired! [*After a pause, listening to the insistent beat of the tom-tom in the distance*] I must 'a put some distance between myself an' dem—runnin' like dat—and yit—dat damn drum sounds jes' de same—nearer, even. Well, I guess I a'most holds my lead anyhow. Dey won't never catch up. [*With a sigh*] If on'y my fool legs stands up. Oh, I'se sorry I evah went in for dis. Dat Emperor's job is sho' hard to shake. [*He looks around him suspiciously.*] How'd this road evah git heah? Good level road, too. I never remembers seein' it befo'. [*Shaking his head apprehensively*] Dese woods is sho' full o' de queerest things at night. [*With a sudden terror*] Lawd God, don't let me see no more o' dem ha'nts! Dey gits my goat! [*Then trying to talk himself into confidence*] Ha'nts! You fool nigger, dey ain't no such things! Don't de Baptist parson tell you dat many times? Is you civilized, or is you like dese ign'rent black niggers heah? Sho'! Dat was all in yo' own head. Wasn't nothin' dere. Wasn't no Jeff! Know what? You jus' get seein' dem things 'cause yo' belly's empty and you's sick wid hunger inside. Hunger 'fects yo' head and yo' eyes. Any fool know dat. [*Then pleading fervently*] But bless God, I don't come across no more o' dem, whatever dey is! [*Then cautiously*] Rest! Don't talk! Rest! You needs it. Den you gits on yo' way again. [*Looking at the moon]* Night's half gone a'most. You hits de coast in de mawning! Den you'se all safe.

[*From the right forward a small gang of* NEGROES *enter. They are dressed in striped convict suits, their heads are shaven, one leg drags limpingly, shackled to a heavy ball and chain. Some carry picks, the others shovels. They are followed by a white man dressed in the uniform of a prison guard. A Winchester rifle is slung across his shoulders and he carries a heavy whip. At a signal from the* GUARD *they stop on the road opposite where* JONES *is sitting.* JONES, *who has been staring up at the sky, unmindful of their noiseless approach, suddenly looks down and sees them. His eyes pop out, he tries to get to his feet and fly, but sinks back, too numbed by fright to move. His voice catches in a choking prayer*]

Lawd Jesus!

[*The* PRISON GUARD *cracks his whip—noiselessly—and at that signal all the convicts start to work on the road. They swing their picks, they shovel, but not a sound comes from their labor. Their movements, like those of* JEFF *in the preceding scene, are those of automatons—rigid, slow, and mechanical. The* PRISON GUARD *points sternly at* JONES *with his whip, motions him to take his place among the other shovelers.* JONES *gets to his feet in a hypnotized stupor. He mumbles subserviently.*]

Yes, suh! Yes, suh! I'se comin'.

[*As he shuffles, dragging one foot, over to his place, he curses under his breath with rage and hatred.*]

God damn yo' soul, I gits even wid you yit, sometime.

[*As if there were a shovel in his hands he goes through weary, mechanical gestures of digging up dirt, and throwing it to the roadside. Suddenly the* GUARD *approaches him angrily, threateningly. He raises his whip and lashes* JONES *viciously across the shoulders with it.* JONES *winces with pain and cowers abjectly. The* GUARD *turns his back on him and walks away contemptuously. Instantly* JONES *straightens up. With arms upraised as if his shovel were a club in his hands he springs murderously at the unsuspecting* GUARD. *In the act of crashing down his shovel on the white man's skull,* JONES *suddenly becomes aware that his hands are empty. He cries despairingly*]

Whar's my shovel? Gimme my shovel till I splits his damn head! [*Appealing to his fellow convicts*] Gimme a shovel, one o' you, fo' God's sake!

[*They stand fixed in motionless attitudes, their eyes on the ground. The* GUARD *seems to wait expectantly, his back turned to the attacker.* JONES *bellows with baffled, terrified rage, tugging frantically at his revolver*]

I kills you, you white debil, if it's de last thing I evah does! Ghost or debil, I kill you again!

[*He frees the revolver and fires point blank at the* GUARD's *back. Instantly the walls of the forest close in from both sides, the road and the figures of the convict gang are blotted out in an enshrouding darkness. The only sounds are a crashing in the underbrush as* JONES *leaps away in mad flight and the throbbing of the tom-tom, still far distant, but increased in volume of sound and rapidity of beat.*]

## SCENE FIVE

SCENE *One o'clock. A large circular clearing, enclosed by the serried ranks of gigantic trunks of tall trees whose tops are lost to view. In the center is a big dead stump worn by time into a curious resemblance to an auction block. The moon floods the clearing with a clear light.* JONES *forces his way in through the forest on the left. He looks wildly about the clearing with hunted, fearful glances. His pants are in tatters, his shoes cut and misshapen, flapping about his feet. He slinks cautiously to the stump in the center and sits down in a tense position, ready for instant flight. Then he holds his head in his hands and rocks back and forth, moaning to himself miserably.*

Oh Lawd, Lawd! Oh Lawd, Lawd! [*Suddenly he throws himself on his knees and raises his clasped hands to the sky—in a voice of agonized pleading.*] Lawd Jesus, heah my prayer! I'se a po' sinner, a po' sinner! I knows I done wrong, I knows it! When I cotches Jeff cheatin' wid loaded dice my anger overcomes me and I kills him dead! Lawd, I done wrong! When dat guard hits me wid de whip, my anger overcomes me, and I kills him dead. Lawd, I done wrong! And down heah whar dese fool bush niggers raises me up to the seat o' de mighty, I steals all I could grab. Lawd, I done wrong! I knows it! I'se sorry! Forgive me, Lawd! Forgive dis po' sinner! [*Then beseeching terrifiedly*] And keep dem away, Lawd! Keep dem away from me! And stop dat drum soundin' in my ears! Dat begin to sound ha'nted, too. [*He gets to his feet, evidently slightly reassured by his prayer—with attempted confidence*] De Lawd'll preserve me from dem ha'nts after dis. [*Sits down on the stump again.*] I ain't skeered o' real men. Let dem come. But dem odders . . . [*He shudders—then looks down at his feet, working his toes inside the shoes—with a groan.*] Oh, my po' feet! Dem shoes ain't no use no more 'ceptin' to hurt. I'se better off widout dem. [*He unlaces them and pulls them off—holds the wrecks of the shoes in his hands and regards them mournfully.*] You was real, A-one patin' leather, too. Look at you now. Emperor, you'se gittin' mighty low!

[*He sits dejectedly and remains with bowed shoulders, staring down at the shoes in his hands as if reluctant to throw them away. While his attention is thus occupied, a crowd of figures silently enter the clearing from all sides. All are dressed in Southern costumes of the period of the fifties of the last century. There are middle-aged men who are evi-*

*dently well-to-do planters. There is one spruce, authoritative individual—the AUCTIONEER. There is a crowd of curious spectators, chiefly young belles and dandies who have come to the slave-market for diversion. All exchange courtly greetings in dumb show and chat silently together. There is something stiff, rigid, unreal, marionettish about their movements. They group themselves about the stump. Finally a batch of slaves are led in from the left by an attendant—three men of different ages, two women, one with a baby in her arms, nursing. They are placed to the left of the stump, beside* JONES.

*The white planters look them over appraisingly as if they were cattle, and exchange judgments on each. The dandies point with their fingers and make witty remarks. The belles titter bewitchingly. All this in silence save for the ominous throb of the tom-tom. The* AUCTIONEER *holds up his hand, taking his place at the stump. The group strain forward attentively. He touches* JONES *on the shoulder peremptorily, motioning for him to stand on the stump—the auction block.*

JONES *looks up, sees the figures on all sides, looks wildly for some opening to escape, sees none, screams and leaps madly to the top of the stump to get as far away from them as possible. He stands there, cowering, paralyzed with horror. The* AUCTIONEER *begins his silent spiel. He points to* JONES, *appeals to the planters to see for themselves. Here is a good field hand, sound in wind and limb as they can see. Very strong still in spite of his being middle-aged. Look at that back. Look at those shoulders. Look at the muscles in his arms and his sturdy legs. Capable of any amount of hard labor. Moreover, of a good disposition, intelligent and tractable. Will any gentleman start the bidding? The* PLANTERS *raise their fingers, make their bids. They are apparently all eager to possess* JONES. *The bidding is lively, the crowd interested. While this has been going on,* JONES *has been seized by the courage of desperation. He dares to look down and around him. Over his face abject terror gives way to mystification, to gradual realization—stutteringly*]

What you all doin', white folks? What's all dis? What you all lookin' at me fo'? What you doin' wid me, anyhow? [*Suddenly convulsed with raging hatred and fear*] Is dis a auction? Is you sellin' me like dey uster befo' de war? [*Jerking out his revolver just as the* AUCTIONEER *knocks him down to one of the planters—glaring from him to the purchaser.*] And *you* sells me? And *you* buys me? I shows you I'se a free nigger, damn yo' souls! [*He fires at the* AUCTIONEER *and at the* PLANTER *with such rapidity that the two shots are almost simultaneous. As if this were a signal the walls of the forest folds in. Only blackness remains and silence broken by* JONES *as he rushes off, crying with fear—and by the quickened, ever louder beat of the tom-tom.*]

# SCENE SIX

SCENE *Three o'clock. A cleared space in the forest. The limbs of the trees meet over it forming a low ceiling about five feet from the ground. The interlocked ropes of creepers reaching upward to entwine the tree trunks give an arched appearance to the sides. The space thus enclosed is like the dark, noisome hold of some ancient vessel. The moonlight is almost completely shut out and only a vague, wan light filters through. There is the noise of someone approaching from the left, stumbling and crawling through the undergrowth.* JONES' *voice is heard between chattering moans.*

Oh, Lawd, what I gwine do now? Ain't got no bullet left on'y de silver one. If mo' o' dem ha'nts come after me, how I gwine skeer dem away? Oh, Lawd, on'y de silver one left—an' I gotta save dat fo' luck. If I shoots dat one I'm a goner sho'! Lawd, it's black heah! Whar's de moon? Oh, Lawd, don't dis night evah come to an end? [*By the sounds, he is feeling his way cautiously forward.*] Dere! Dis feels like a clear space. I gotta lie down an' rest. I don't care if dem niggers does cotch me. I gotta rest.

[*He is well forward now where his figure can be dimly made out. His pants have been so torn away that what is left of them is no better than a breech cloth. He flings himself full length, face downward on the ground, panting with exhaustion. Gradually it seems to grow lighter in the enclosed space and two rows of seated figures can be seen behind* JONES. *They are sitting in crumbled, despairing attitudes, hunched, facing one another with their backs touching the forest walls as if they were shackled to them. All are Negroes, naked save for loin cloths. At first they are silent and motionless. Then they begin to sway slowly forward toward each other and back again in unison, as if they were laxly letting themselves follow the long roll of a ship at sea. At the same time, a low, melancholy murmur rises among them, increasing gradually by rhythmic degrees which seem to be directed and controlled by the throb of the tom-tom in the distance, to a long, tremulous wail of despair that reaches a certain pitch, unbearably acute, then falls by slow gradations of tone into silence and is taken up again.* JONES *starts, looks up, sees the figures, and throws himself down again to shut out the sight. A shudder of terror shakes his whole body as the wail rises up about him again. But the next time, his voice, as if under some uncanny compulsion, starts with the others. As their chorus lifts he rises to a sitting posture similar to the others, swaying back and forth. His voice reaches the highest pitch of sorrow, of desolation. The light fades out, the other voices cease, and only darkness is left.* JONES *can be heard scrambling to his feet and running off, his voice sinking down the scale and receding as he moves farther and farther away in the forest. The tom-tom beats louder, quicker, with a more insistent, triumphant pulsation.*]

# SCENE SEVEN

SCENE *Five o'clock. The foot of a gigantic tree by the edge of a great river. A rough structure of boulders, like an altar, is by the tree. The raised river bank is in the nearer background. Beyond this the surface of the river spreads out, brilliant and unruffled in the moonlight, blotted out and merged into a veil of bluish mist in the distance.* JONES' *voice is heard from the left rising and falling in the long, despairing wail of the chained slaves, to the rhythmic beat of the tom-tom. As his voice sinks into silence, he enters the open space. The expression of his face is fixed and stony, his eyes have an obsessed glare, he moves with a strange deliberation like a sleepwalker or one in a trance. He looks around at the tree, the rough stone altar, the moonlit surface of the river beyond, and passes his hand over his head with a vague gesture of puzzled bewilderment. Then, as if in obedience to some obscure impulse, he sinks into a kneeling, devotional posture before the altar. Then he*

*seems to come to himself partly, to have an
uncertain realization of what he is doing, for
he straightens up and stares about him horrifiedly—in an incoherent mumble*

What—what is I doin'? What is—dis place? Seems like—seems like I know dat tree—an' dem stones—an' de river. I remember—seems like I ben heah befo'. [*Tremblingly*] Oh, Gorry, I'se skeered in dis place! I'se skeered! Oh, Lawd, pertect dis sinner!

[*Crawling away from the altar, he cowers close to the ground, his face hidden, his shoulders heaving with sobs of hysterical fright. From behind the trunk of the tree, as if he had sprung out of it, the figure of the* CONGO WITCH-DOCTOR *appears. He is wizened and old, naked except for the fur of some small animal tied about his waist, its bushy tail hanging down in front. His body is stained all over a bright red. Antelope horns are on each side of his head, branching upward. In one hand he carries a bone rattle, in the other a charm stick with a bunch of white cockatoo feathers tied to the end. A great number of glass beads and bone ornaments are about his neck, ears, wrists, and ankles. He struts noiselessly with a queer prancing step to a position in the clear ground between* JONES *and the altar. Then with a preliminary, summoning stamp of his foot on the earth, he begins to dance and to chant. As if in response to his summons the beating of the tom-tom grows to a fierce, exultant boom whose throbs seem to fill the air with vibrating rhythm.* JONES *looks up, starts to spring to his feet, reaches a half-kneeling, half-squatting position and remains rigidly fixed there, paralyzed with awed fascination by this new apparition. The* WITCH-DOCTOR *sways, stamping with his foot, his bone rattle clicking the time. His voice rises and falls in a weird, monotonous croon, without articulate word divisions. Gradually his dance becomes clearly one of a narrative in pantomime, his croon is an incantation, a charm to allay the fierceness of some implacable deity demanding sacrifice. He flees, he is pursued by devils, he hides, he flees again. Ever wilder and wilder becomes his flight, nearer and nearer draws the pursuing evil, more and more the spirit of terror gains possession of him. His croon, rising to intensity, is punctuated by shrill cries.* JONES *has become completely hypnotized. His voice joins in the incantation, in the cries, he beats time with his hands and sways his body to and fro from the waist. The whole spirit and meaning of the dance has entered into him, has become his spirit. Finally the theme of the pantomime halts on a howl of despair, and is taken up again in a note of savage hope. There is a salvation. The forces of evil demand sacrifice. They must be appeased. The* WITCH-DOCTOR *points with his wand to the sacred tree, to the river beyond, to the altar, and finally to* JONES *with a ferocious command.* JONES *seems to sense the meaning of this. It is he who must offer himself for sacrifice. He beats his forehead abjectly to the ground, moaning hysterically.*]

Mercy, Oh Lawd! Mercy! Mercy on dis po' sinner.

[*The* WITCH-DOCTOR *springs to the river bank. He stretches out his arms and calls to some god within its depths. Then he starts backward slowly, his arms remaining out. A huge head of a crocodile appears over the bank and its eyes, glittering greenly, fasten upon* JONES. *He stares into them fascinatedly. The* WITCH-DOCTOR *prances up to him, touches him with his wand, motions with hideous command toward the waiting monster.* JONES *squirms on his belly nearer and nearer, moaning continually.*]

Mercy, Lawd! Mercy!

[*The crocodile heaves more of his enormous hulk onto the land.* JONES *squirms toward him. The* WITCH-DOCTOR'S *voice shrills out in furious exultation, the tom-tom beats madly.* JONES *cries out in a fierce, exhausted spasm of anguished pleading.*]

Lawd, save me! Lawd Jesus, heah my prayer!

[*Immediately, in answer to his prayer, comes the thought of the one bullet left him. He snatches at his hip, shouting defiantly.*]

De silver bullet! You don't git me yit!

[*He fires at the green eyes in front of him. The head of the crocodile sinks back behind the river bank, the* WITCH-DOCTOR *springs behind the sacred tree and disappears.* JONES *lies with his face to the ground, his arms outstretched, whimpering with fear as the throb of the tom-tom fills the silence about him with a somber pulsation, a baffled but revengeful power.*]

# SCENE EIGHT

SCENE *Dawn. Same as Scene Two, the dividing line
of forest and plain. The nearest tree trunks
are dimly revealed but the forest behind them
is still a mass of glooming shadows. The tom-
tom seems on the very spot, so loud and con-
tinuously vibrating are its beats. LEM enters
from the left, followed by a small squad of his
soldiers, and by the Cockney trader, SMITHERS.
LEM is a heavy-set, ape-faced old savage of the
extreme African type, dressed only in a loin
cloth. A revolver and cartridge belt are about
his waist. His soldiers are in different degrees
of rag-concealed nakedness. All wear broad
palm-leaf hats. Each one carries a rifle.
SMITHERS is the same as in Scene One. One of
the soldiers, evidently a tracker, is peering
about keenly on the ground. He grunts and
points at the spot where JONES entered the
forest. LEM and SMITHERS come to look.*

SMITHERS [*After a glance, turns away in disgust*]
That's where 'e went in right enough. Much good

it'll do yer. 'E's miles orf by this an' safe to the Coast, damn 'is 'ide! I tole yer yer'd lose 'im, didn't I?—wastin' the 'ole bloomin' night beatin' yer bloody drum and castin' yer silly spells! Gawd blimey, wot a pack!

LEM [*Gutturally*] We cotch him. You see. [*He makes a motion to his soldiers who squat down on their haunches in a semicircle.*]

SMITHERS [*Exasperatedly*] Well, ain't yer goin' in an' 'unt 'im in the woods? What the 'ell's the good of waitin'?

LEM [*Imperturbably—squatting down himself*] We cotch him.

SMITHERS [*Turning away from him contemptuously*] Aw! Garn! 'E's a better man than the lot o' you put together. I 'ates the sight of 'im but I'll say that for 'im. [*A sound of snapping twigs comes from the forest. The soldiers jump to their feet, cocking their rifles alertly.* LEM *remains sitting with an imperturbable expression, but listening intently. The sound from the woods is repeated.* LEM *makes a quick signal with his hand. His followers creep quickly but noiselessly into the forest, scattering so that each enters at a different spot.*]

SMITHERS [*In the silence that follows—in a contemptuous whisper*] You ain't thinkin' that would be 'im, I 'ope?

LEM [*Calmly*] We cotch him.

SMITHERS Blarsted fat 'eads! [*Then after a second's thought—wonderingly*] Still an' all, it might 'appen. If 'e lost 'is bloody way in these stinkin' woods 'e'd likely turn in a circle without 'is knowin' it. They all does.

LEM [*Peremptorily*] Sssh! [*The reports of several rifles sound from the forest, followed a second later by savage, exultant yells. The beating of the tom-tom abruptly ceases.* LEM *looks up at the white man with a grin of satisfaction.*] We cotch him. Him dead.

SMITHERS [*With a snarl*] 'Ow d'yer know it's 'im an' 'ow d'yer know 'e's dead?

LEM My mens dey got 'um silver bullets. Dey kill him shore.

SMITHERS [*Astonished*] They got silver bullets?

LEM Lead bullet no kill him. He got um strong charm. I cook um money, make um silver bullet, make um strong charm, too.

SMITHERS [*Light breaking upon him*] So that's wot you was up to all night, wot? You was scared to put after 'im till you'd moulded silver bullets, eh?

LEM [*Simply stating a fact*] Yes. Him got strong charm. Lead no good.

SMITHERS [*Slapping his thigh and guffawing*] Haw-haw! If yer don't beat all 'ell! [*Then recovering himself—scornfully*] I'll bet yer it ain't 'im they shot at all, yer bleedin' looney!

LEM [*Calmly*] Dey come bring him now. [*The soldiers come out of the forest, carrying* JONES' *limp body. There is a little reddish-purple hole under his left breast. He is dead. They carry him to* LEM, *who examines his body with great satisfaction.* SMITHERS *leans over his shoulder—in a tone of frightened awe.*] Well, they did for yer right enough,

Jonsey, me lad! Dead as a 'erring! [*Mockingly*] Where's yer 'igh an' mighty airs now, yer bloomin' Majesty? [*Then with a grin*] Silver bullets! Gawd blimey, but yer died in the 'eight o' style, any'ow! [LEM *makes a motion to the soldiers to carry the body out left.* SMITHERS *speaks to him sneeringly.*]

SMITHERS And I s'pose you think it's yer bleedin' charms and yer silly beatin' the drum that made 'im run in a circle when 'e'd lost 'imself, don't yer? [*But* LEM *makes no reply, does not seem to hear the question, walks out left after his men.* SMITHERS *looks after him with contemptuous scorn.*] Stupid as 'ogs, the lot of 'em! Blarsted niggers!

[*The curtain falls.*]

# ANNA CHRISTIE

---

*A Play in Four Acts*

# CHARACTERS

"JOHNNY-THE-PRIEST"
TWO LONGSHOREMEN
A POSTMAN
LARRY, *bartender*
CHRIS CHRISTOPHERSON,
    *captain of the barge* Simeon Winthrop
MARTHY OWEN
ANNA CHRISTOPHERSON, *Chris's daughter*
THREE MEN OF A STEAMER'S CREW
MAT BURKE, *a stoker*
JOHNSON, *deckhand on the barge*

# SCENES

**Act I**     "Johnny-the-Priest's saloon near the water front, New York City.

**Act II**     The barge, *Simeon Winthrop*, at anchor in the harbor of Provincetown, Mass. Ten days later.

**Act III**     Cabin of the barge, at dock in Boston. A week later.

**Act IV**     The same. Two days later.

# ANNA CHRISTIE

---

## ACT ONE

SCENE *"JOHNNY-THE-PRIEST'S" saloon near South Street, New York City. The stage is divided into two sections, showing a small back room on the right. On the left, forward, of the barroom, a large window looking out on the street. Beyond it, the main entrance—a double swinging door. Farther back, another window. The bar runs from left to right nearly the whole length of the rear wall. In back of the bar, a small showcase displaying a few bottles of case goods, for which there is evidently little call. The remainder of the rear space in front of the large mirrors is occupied by half-barrels of cheap whisky of the "nickel-a-shot" variety, from which the liquor is drawn by means of spigots. On the right is an open doorway leading to the back room. In the back room are four round wooden tables with five chairs grouped about each. In the rear, a family entrance opening on a side street.*

*It is late afternoon of a day in fall*

*As the curtain rises, JOHNNY is discovered. "JOHNNY-THE-PRIEST" deserves his nickname. With his pale, thin, clean-shaven face, mild blue eyes and white hair, a cassock would seem more suited to him than the apron he wears. Neither his voice nor his general manner dispel this illusion which has made him a personage of the water front. They are soft and bland. But beneath all his mildness one senses the man behind the mask—cynical, callous, hard as nails. He is lounging at ease behind the bar, a pair of spectacles on his nose, reading an evening paper.*

*Two longshoremen enter from the street, wearing their working aprons, the button of the union pinned conspicuously on the caps pulled sideways on their heads at an aggressive angle.*

FIRST LONGSHOREMAN [*As they range themselves at the bar*] Gimme a shock. Number Two. [*He tosses a coin on the bar.*]

SECOND LONGSHOREMAN Same here. [JOHNNY *sets two glasses of barrel whisky before them.*]

FIRST LONGSHOREMAN Here's luck! [*The other nods. They gulp down their whisky.*]

SECOND LONGSHOREMAN [*Putting money on the bar*] Give us another.

FIRST LONGSHOREMAN Gimme a scoop this time—lager and porter. I'm dry.

SECOND LONGSHOREMAN Same here. [JOHNNY *draws the lager and porter and sets the big, foaming schooners before them. They drink down half the contents and start to talk together hurriedly in low tones. The door on the left is swung open and* LARRY *enters. He is a boyish, red-cheeked, rather good-looking young fellow of twenty or so.*]

LARRY [*Nodding to* JOHNNY—*cheerily*] Hello, boss.

JOHNNY Hello, Larry. [*With a glance at his watch*] Just on time. [LARRY *goes to the right behind the bar, takes off his coat, and puts on an apron.*]

FIRST LONGSHOREMAN [*Abruptly*] Let's drink up and get back to it. [*They finish their drinks and go out left.* THE POSTMAN *enters as they leave. He exchanges nods with* JOHNNY *and throws a letter on the bar.*]

THE POSTMAN Addressed care of you, Johnny. Know him?

JOHNNY [*Picks up the letter, adjusting his spectacles.* LARRY *comes and peers over his shoulders.* JOHNNY *reads very slowly.*] Christopher Christopherson.

THE POSTMAN [*Helpfully*] Square-head name.

LARRY Old Chris—that's who.

JOHNNY Oh, sure. I was forgetting Chris carried a hell of a name like that. Letters come here for him sometimes before, I remember now. Long time ago, though.

THE POSTMAN It'll get him all right then?

JOHNNY Sure thing. He comes here whenever he's in port.

THE POSTMAN [*Turning to go*] Sailor, eh?

JOHNNY [*With a grin*] Captain of a coal barge.

THE POSTMAN [*Laughing*] Some job! Well, s'long.

JOHNNY S'long. I'll see he gets it. [THE POSTMAN *goes out.* JOHNNY *scrutinizes the letter.*] You got good eyes, Larry. Where's it from?

LARRY [*After a glance*] St. Paul. That'll be in Minnesota, I'm thinkin'. Looks like a woman's writing, too, the old divil!

JOHNNY He's got a daughter somewheres out West, I think he told me once. [*He puts the letter on the cash register.*] Come to think of it, I ain't seen old Chris in a dog's age. [*Putting his overcoat on, he comes around the end of the bar.*] Guess I'll be gettin' home. See you tomorrow.

LARRY Good-night to ye, boss. [*As* JOHNNY *goes toward the street door, it is pushed open and* CHRISTOPHER CHRISTOPHERSON *enters. He is a short, squat, broad-shouldered man of about fifty, with a round, weather-beaten, red face from which his light blue eyes peer shortsightedly, twinkling with a simple good humor. His large mouth, overhung by a thick, drooping, yellow mustache, is childishly self-willed and weak, of an obstinate kindliness. A thick neck is jammed like a post into the heavy trunk of his body. His arms with their big, hairy, freckled hands, and his stumpy legs terminating in large flat feet, are awkwardly short and muscular. He walks with a clumsy, rolling gait. His voice, when not raised in a hollow boom, is toned down to a sly, confidential half-whisper with something vaguely plaintive in its quality. He is dressed in a wrinkled, ill-fitting dark suit of shore clothes, and wears a faded cap of gray cloth over his mop of grizzled, blond hair. Just now his face beams with a too-blissful happiness, and he has evidently been drinking. He reaches his hand out to* JOHNNY.]

CHRIS  Hello, Yohnny! Have a drink on me. Come on, Larry. Give us drink. Have one yourself. [*Putting his hand in his pocket*] Ay gat money—plenty money. . . .

JOHNNY [*Shakes* CHRIS *by the hand*]  Speak of the devil. We was just talkin' about you.

LARRY [*Coming to the end of the bar*]  Hello, Chris. Put it there. [*They shake hands.*]

CHRIS [*Beaming*]  Give us drink.

JOHNNY [*With a grin*]  You got a half snootful now. Where'd you get it?

CHRIS [*Grinning*]  Oder fallar on oder barge—Irish fallar—he gat bottle vhisky and we drank it, yust us two. Dot vhisky gat kick, by yingo! Ay yust come ashore. Give us drink, Larry. Ay vas little drunk, not much. Yust feel good. [*He laughs and commences to sing in a nasal, high-pitched quaver.*] "My Yosephine, come aboard de ship. Long time
  Ay vait for you.
De moon, she shi-i-i-ine. She looka yus like you.
    Tchee-tchee, tchee-tchee, tchee-tchee, tchee-tchee."
[*To the accompaniment of this last he waves his hand as if he were conducting an orchestra.*]

JOHNNY [*With a laugh*]  Same old Yosie, eh Chris?

CHRIS  You don't know good song when you hear

him. Italian fallar on oder barge, he learn me dat. Give us drink. [*He throws change on the bar.*]

LARRY [*With a professional air*] What's your pleasure, gentlemen?

JOHNNY  Small beer, Larry.

CHRIS  Vhisky—Number Two.

LARRY [*As he gets their drinks*]  I'll take a cigar on you.

CHRIS [*Lifting his glass*]  Skoal! [*He drinks.*]

JOHNNY  Drink hearty.

CHRIS [*Immediately*]  Have oder drink.

JOHNNY  No. Some other time. Got to go home now. So you've just landed? Where are you in from this time?

CHRIS  Norfolk. Ve make slow voyage—dirty vedder—yust fog, fog, fog, all bloody time! [*There is an insistent ring from the doorbell at the family entrance in the back room.* CHRIS *gives a start—hurriedly.*] Ay go open, Larry. Ay forgat. It vas Marthy. She come with me. [*He goes into the back room.*]

LARRY [*With a chuckle*]  He's still got that same cow livin' with him, the old fool!

JOHNNY [*With a grin*]  A sport, Chris is. Well, I'll beat it home. S'long. [*He goes to the street door.*]

LARRY  So long, boss.

JOHNNY  Oh—don't forget to give him his letter.

LARRY  I won't. [JOHNNY *goes out. In the meantime,* CHRIS *has opened the family entrance door, admitting* MARTHY. *She might be forty or fifty. Her jowly mottled face, with its thick red nose, is streaked with interlacing purple veins. Her thick, gray hair is piled anyhow in a greasy mop on top of her round head. Her figure is flabby and fat; her breath comes in wheezy gasps; she speaks in a loud, mannish voice, punctuated by explosions of hoarse laughter. But there still twinkles in her blood-shot eyes a youthful lust for life which hard usage has failed to stifle, a sense of humor mocking, but good-tempered. She wears a man's cap, doublebreasted man's jacket, and a grimy, calico skirt. Her bare feet are encased in a man's brogans several sizes too large for her, which gives her a shuffling, wobbly gait.]*

MARTHY [*Grumblingly*] What yuh tryin' to do, Dutchy—keep me standin' out there all day? [*She comes forward and sits at the table in the right corner, front.*]

CHRIS [*Mollifyingly*] Ay'm sorry, Marthy, Ay talk to Yohnny. Ay forgat. What you goin' take for drink?

MARTHY [*Appeased*] Gimme a scoop of lager an' ale.

CHRIS Ay go bring him back. [*He returns to the bar.*] Lager and ale for Marthy, Larry. Vhisky for me. [*He throws change on the bar.*]

LARRY Right you are. [*Then remembering, he takes the letter from in back of the bar.*] Here's a letter for you—from St. Paul, Minnesota—and a lady's writin'. [*He grins.*]

CHRIS [*Quickly—taking it*] Oh, den it come from my daughter, Anna. She live dere. [*He turns the letter over in his hands uncertainly.*] Ay don't gat letter from Anna—must be a year.

LARRY [*Jokingly*] That's a fine fairy tale to be tellin'—your daughter! Sure I'll bet it's some bum.

CHRIS [*Soberly*] No. Dis come from Anna. [*Engrossed by the letter in his hand—uncertainly*] By golly, Ay tank Ay'm too drunk for read dis letter from Anna. Ay tank Ay sat down for a minute. You bring drinks in back room, Larry. [*He goes into the room on right.*]

MARTHY [*Angrily*] Where's my lager an' ale, yuh big stiff?

CHRIS [*Preoccupied*] Larry bring him. [*He sits down opposite her.* LARRY *brings in the drinks and sets them on the table. He and* MARTHY *exchange nods of recognition.* LARRY *stands looking at* CHRIS *curiously.* MARTHY *takes a long draught of her schooner and heaves a huge sigh of satisfaction, wiping her mouth with the back of her hand.* CHRIS *stares at the letter for a moment—slowly opens it, and, squinting his eyes, commences to read laboriously, his lips moving as he spells out the words. As he reads his face lights up with an expression of mingled joy and bewilderment.*]

LARRY Good news?

MARTHY [*Her curiosity also aroused*] What's that yuh got—a letter, fur Gawd's sake?

CHRIS [*Pauses for a moment, after finishing the letter, as if to let the news sink in—then suddenly pounds his fist on the table with happy excitement*] Py yiminy! Yust tank, Anna say she's comin' here right avay! She gat sick on yob in St. Paul, she say. It's short letter, don't tal me much more'n dat. [*Beaming*] Py golly, dat's good news all at one time for ole fallar! [*Then turning to* MARTHY, *rather shamefacedly.*] You know, Marthy, Ay've tole you Ay don't see my Anna since she vas little gel in Sveden five year ole.

MARTHY How old'll she be now?

CHRIS She must be—lat me see—she must be twenty year ole, py Yo!

LARRY [*Surprised*] You've not seen her in fifteen years?

CHRIS [*Suddenly growing somber—in a low tone*] No. Ven she vas little gel, Ay vas bosun on vindjammer. Ay never gat home only few time dem year. Ay'm fool sailor fallar. My voman—Anna's mother —she gat tired vait all time Sveden for me ven Ay don't never come. She come dis country, bring Anna, dey go out Minnesota, live with her cousins on farm. Den ven her mo'der die ven Ay vas on voyage, Ay tank it's better dem cousins keep Anna. Ay tank it's better Anna live on farm, den she don't know dat ole davil, sea she don't know fa'der like me.

LARRY [*With a wink at* MARTY] This girl, now, 'll be marryin a sailor herself, likely. It's in the blood.

CHRIS [*Suddenly springing to his feet and smashing his fist on the table in a rage*] No, py God! She don't do dat!

MARTHY [*Grasping her schooner hastily—angrily*] Hey, look out, yuh nut! Wanta spill my suds for me?

LARRY [*Amazed*] Oho, what's up with you? Ain't you a sailor yourself now, and always been?

CHRIS [*Slowly*] Dat's yust vhy Ay say it. [*Forcing a smile*] Sailor vas all right fallar, but not for marry gel. No, Ay know dat. Anna's mo'der, she know it, too.

LARRY [*As* CHRIS *remains sunk in gloomy reflection*] When is your daughter comin'? Soon?

CHRIS [*Roused*] Py yiminy, Ay forgat. [*Reads through the letter hurriedly.*] She say she come right avay, dat's all.

LARRY She'll maybe be comin' here to look for you, I s'pose. [*He returns to the bar, whistling. Left alone with* MARTHY, *who stares at him with a twinkle of malicious humor in her eyes,* CHRIS *suddenly becomes desperately ill-at-ease. He fidgets, then gets up hurriedly.*]

CHRIS Ay gat speak with Larry. Ay be right back. [*Mollifyingly*] Ay bring you oder drink.

MARTHY [*Emptying her glass*] Sure. That's me. [*As he retreats with the glass she guffaws after him derisively.*]

CHRIS [*To* LARRY *in an alarmed whisper*] Py yingo, Ay gat gat Marthy shore off barge before Anna come! Anna raise hell if she find dat out. Marthy raise hell, too, for go, py golly!

LARRY [*With a chuckle*] Serve ye right, ye old divil—havin' a woman at your age!

CHRIS [*Scratching his head in a quandary*] You tal me lie for tal Marthy, Larry, so's she gat off barge quick.

LARRY She knows your daughter's comin'. Tell her to get the hell out of it.

CHRIS No. Ay don't like make her feel bad.

LARRY You're an old mush! Keep your girl away from the barge, then. She'll likely want to stay ashore anyway. [*Curiously*] What does she work at, your Anna?

ANNA CHRISTIE 69

CHRIS She stay on dem cousins farm till two year ago. Dan she gat yob nurse gel in St. Paul. [*Then shaking his head resolutely*] But Ay don't vant for her gat yob now. Ay vant for her stay with me.

LARRY [*Scornfully*] On a coal barge! She'll not like that, I'm thinkin'.

MARTHY [*Shouts from next room*] Don't I get that bucket o' suds, Dutchy?

CHRIS [*Startled—in apprehensive confusion*] Yes, Ay come, Marthy.

LARRY [*Drawing the lager and ale, hands it to Chris—laughing.*] Now you're in for it! You'd better tell her straight to get out!

CHRIS [*Shaking in his boots*] Py golly. [*He takes her drink in to* MARTHY *and sits down at the table. She sips it in silence.* LARRY *moves quietly close to the partition to listen, grinning with expectation.* CHRIS *seems on the verge of speaking, hesitates, gulps down his whisky desperately as if seeking courage. He attempts to whistle a few bars of "Yosephine" with careless bravado, but the whistle peters out futilely.* MARTHY *stares at him keenly, taking in his embarrassment with a malicious twinkle of amusement in her eye.* CHRIS *clears his throat.*] Marthy——

MARTHY [*Aggressively*] Wha's that? [*Then, pretending to fly into a rage, her eyes enjoying* CHRIS' *misery.*] I'm wise to what's in back of your nut, Dutchy. Yuh want to git rid o' me, huh?—now she's comin'. Gimme the bum's rush ashore, huh? Lemme tell yuh, Dutchy, there ain't a square-head workin' on a boat man enough to git away with that. Don't start nothin' yuh can't finish!

CHRIS [*Miserably*] Ay don't start nutting, Marthy.

MARTHY [*Glares at him for a second—then cannot control a burst of laughter*] Ho-ho! yuh're a scream, Square-head—an honest-ter-Gawd knockout! Ho-ho! [*She wheezes, panting for breath.*]

CHRIS [*With childish pique*] Ay don't see nutting for laugh at.

MARTHY Take a slant in the mirror and yuh'll see. Ho-ho! [*Recovering from her mirth—chuckling, scornfully.*] A square-head tryin' to kid Marthy Owen at this late day!—after me campin' with barge men the last twenty years. I'm wise to the game, up, down, and sideways. I ain't been born and dragged up on the water front for nothin'. Think I'd make trouble, huh? Not me! I'll pack up me duds an' beat it. I'm quittin' yuh, get me! I'm tellin' yuh I'm sick of stickin with yuh, and I'm leavin' yuh flat, see? There's plenty of other guys on other barges waitin' for me. Always was, I always found. [*She claps the astonished* CHRIS *on the back.*] So cheer up, Dutchy! I'll be offen the barge before she comes. You'll be rid o' me for good—and me o' you—good riddance for both of us. Ho-ho!

CHRIS [*Seriously*] Ay don' tank dat. You vas good gel, Marthy.

MARTHY [*Grinning*] Good girl? Aw, can the bull! Well, yuh treated me square, yuhself. So it's fifty-fifty. Nobody's sore at nobody. We're still good frien's, huh? [LARRY *returns to bar.*]

CHRIS [*Beaming now that he sees his troubles disappearing*] Yes, py golly.

MARTHY That's the talkin'! In all my time I tried never to split with a guy with no hard feelin's. But what was yuh so scared about—that I'd kick up a row? That ain't Marthy's way. [*Scornfully*] Think I'd break my heart to lose yuh? Commit suicide, huh? Ho-ho! Gawd! The world's full o' men if that's all I'd worry about! [*Then with a grin, after emptying her glass.*] Blow me to another scoop, huh? I'll drink your kid's health for yuh.

CHRIS [*Eagerly*] Sure tang. Ay go gat him. [*He takes the two glasses into the bar.*] Oder drink. Same for both.

LARRY [*Getting the drinks and putting them on the bar*] She's not such a bad lot, that one.

CHRIS [*Jovially*] She's good gel, Ay tal you! Py golly, Ay calabrate now! Give me vhisky here at bar, too. [*He puts down money.* LARRY *serves him.*] You have drink, Larry.

LARRY [*Virtuously*] You know I never touch it.

CHRIS You don't know what you miss. Skoal! [*He drinks—then begins to sing loudly*] "My Yosephine, come board de ship——" [*He picks up the drinks for* MARTHY *and himself and walks unsteadily into the back room, singing*] "De moon, she shi-i-i-ine. She looks yust like you. Tchee-tchee, tchee-tchee, tchee-tchee, tchee-tchee."

MARTHY [*Grinning, hands to ears*] Gawd!

CHRIS [*Sitting down*] Ay'm good singer, yes? Ve drink, eh? Skoal! Ay calabrate! [*He drinks.*] Ay calabrate 'cause Anna's coming home You know,

Marthy, Ay never write for her to come, 'cause Ay tank Ay'm no good for her. But all time Ay hope like hell some day she vant for see me and den she come. And dat's vay it happen now, py yiminy! [*His face beaming*] What you tank she look like, Marthy? Ay bet you she's fine, good, strong gel, pooty like hell! Living on farm made her like dat. And Ay bet you some day she marry good, steady land fallar here in East, have home all her own, have kits—and dan Ay'm ole grandfader, py golly! And Ay go visit dem every time Ay gat in port near! [*Bursting with joy*] By yiminy crickens, Ay calabrate dat! [*Shouts*] Bring oder drink, Larry! [*He smashes his fist on the table with a bang.*]

LARRY [*Coming in from bar—irritably*] Easy there! Don't be breakin' the table, you old goat!

CHRIS [*By way of reply, grins foolishly, and begins to sing*]

"My Yosephine, come board de ship——"

MARTHY [*Touching* CHRIS' *arm persuasively*] You're soused to the ears, Dutchy. Go out and put a feed into you. It'll sober you up. [*Then as* CHRIS *shakes his head obstinately*] Listen, yuh old nut! Yuh don't know what time your kid's liable to show up. Yuh want to be sober when she comes, don't yuh?

CHRIS [*Aroused—gets unsteadily to his feet*] Py golly, yes.

LARRY That's good sense for you. A good beef stew'll fix you. Go round the corner.

CHRIS All right. Ay be back soon, Marthy.

[CHRIS *goes through the bar and out the street door.*]

LARRY He'll come round all right with some grub in him.

MARTHY Sure. [LARRY *goes back to the bar and resumes his newspaper.* MARTHY *sips what is left of her schooner reflectively. There is the ring of the family entrance bell.* LARRY *comes to the door and opens it a trifle—then, with a puzzled expression, pulls it wide.* ANNA CHRISTOPHERSON *enters. She is a tall, blond, fully-developed girl of twenty, handsome after a large, Viking-daughter fashion but now run down in health and plainly showing all the outward evidences of belonging to the world's oldest profession. Her youthful face is already hard and cynical beneath its layer of make-up. Her clothes are the tawdry finery of peasant stock turned prostitute. She comes and sinks wearily in a chair by the table, left front.*]

ANNA Gimme a whisky—ginger ale on the side. [*Then, as* LARRY *turns to go, forcing a winning smile at him.*] And don't be stingy, baby.

LARRY [*Sarcastically*] Shall I serve it in a pail?

ANNA [*With a hard laugh*] That suits me down to the ground. [LARRY *goes into the bar. The two women size each other up with frank stares.* LARRY *comes back with the drink which he sets before* ANNA *and returns to the bar again.* ANNA *downs her drink at a gulp. Then, after a moment, as the alcohol begins to rouse her, she turns to* MARTHY *with a friendly smile.*] Gee, I needed that bad, all right, all right!

MARTHY [*Nodding her head sympathetically*] Sure—yuh look all in. Been on a bat?

ANNA No—traveling—day and a half on the train. Had to sit up all night in the dirty coach, too. Gawd, I thought I'd never get here!

MARTHY [*With a start—looking at her intently*] Where'd yuh come from, huh?

ANNA St. Paul—out in Minnesota.

MARTHY [*Staring at her in amazement—slowly*] So—yuh're—— [*She suddenly bursts out into hoarse, ironical laughter.*] Gawd!

ANNA All the way from Minnesota, sure. [*Flaring up*] What you laughing at? Me?

MARTHY [*Hastily*] No, honest, kid. I was thinkin' of somethin' else.

ANNA [*Mollified—with a smile*] Well, I wouldn't blame you, at that. Guess I do look rotten—yust out of the hospital two weeks. I'm going to have another 'ski. What d'you say? Have something on me?

MARTHY Sure I will. T'anks. [*She calls*] Hey, Larry! Little service! [*He comes in.*]

ANNA Same for me.

MARTHY Same here. [LARRY *takes their glasses and goes out.*]

ANNA Why don't you come sit over here, be sociable. I'm a dead stranger in this burg—and I ain't spoke a word with no one since day before yesterday.

MARTHY Sure thing. [*She shuffles over to* ANNA's *table and sits down opposite her.* LARRY *brings the drinks and* ANNA *pays him.*]

ANNA Skoal! Here's how! [*She drinks.*]

MARTHY  Here's luck! [*She takes a gulp from her schooner.*]

ANNA [*Taking a package of Sweet Caporal cigarettes from her bag*]  Let you smoke in here, won't they?

MARTHY [*Doubtfully*]  Sure. [*Then with evident anxiety*] On'y trow it away if yuh hear someone comin'.

ANNA [*Lighting one and taking a deep inhale*] Gee, they're fussy in this dump, ain't they? [*She puffs, staring at the table top.* MARTHY *looks her over with a new penetrating interest, taking in every detail of her face.* ANNA *suddenly becomes conscious of this appraising stare—resentfully.*] Ain't nothing wrong with me, is there? You're looking hard enough.

MARTHY [*Irritated by the other's tone—scornfully*] Ain't got to look much. I got your number the minute you stepped in the door.

ANNA [*Her eyes narrowing*]  Ain't you smart! Well, I got yours, too, without no trouble. You're me forty years from now. That's you! [*She gives a hard little laugh.*]

MARTHY [*Angrily*]  Is that so? Well, I'll tell you straight, kiddo, that Marthy Owen never—— [*She catches herself up short—with a grin.*] What are you and me scrappin' over? Let's cut it out, huh? Me, I don't want no hard feelin's with no one. [*Extending her hand*] Shake and forget it, huh?

ANNA [*Shakes her hand gladly*]  Only too glad to. I ain't looking for trouble. Let's have 'nother. What d'you say?

MARTHY [*Shaking her head*] Not for mine. I'm full up. And you—— Had anythin' to eat lately?

ANNA  Not since this morning on the train.

MARTHY  Then yuh better go easy on it, hadn'* yuh?

ANNA [*After a moment's hesitation*] Guess you're right. I got to meet someone, too. But my nerves is on edge after that rotten trip.

MARTHY  Yuh said yuh was just outa the hospital?

ANNA  Two weeks ago [*Leaning over to* MARTHY *confidentially*] The joint I was in out in St. Paul got raided. That was the start. The judge give all us girls thirty days. The others didn't seem to mind being in the cooler much. Some of 'em was used to it. But me, I couldn't stand it. It got my goat right —couldn't eat or sleep or nothing. I never could stand being caged up nowheres. I got good and sick and they had to send me to the hospital. It was nice there. I was sorry to leave it, honest!

MARTHY [*After a slight pause*] Did yuh say yuh got to meet someone here?

ANNA  Yes. Oh, not what you mean. It's my Old Man I got to meet. Honest! It's funny, too. I ain't seen him since I was a kid—don't even know what he looks like—yust had a letter every now and then. This was always the only address he give me to write him back. He's yanitor of some building here now—used to be a sailor.

MARTHY [*Astonished*] Janitor!

ANNA  Sure. And I was thinking maybe, seeing he ain't never done a thing for me in my life, he might be willing to stake me to a room and eats till I get rested up. [*Wearily*] Gee, I sure need that rest! I'm knocked out. [*Then resignedly*] But I ain't expecting much from him. Give you a kick when you're down, that's what all men do. [*With sudden passion*] Men, I hate 'em—all of 'em! And I don't expect he'll turn out no better than the rest. [*Then with sudden interest*] Say, do you hang out around this dump much?

MARTHY   Oh, off and on.

ANNA   Then maybe you know him—my Old Man —or at least seen him?

MARTHY   It ain't old Chris, is it?

ANNA   Old Chris?

MARTHY   Chris Christopherson, his full name is.

ANNA [*Excitedly*]   Yes, that's him! Anna Christopherson—that's my real name—only out there I called myself Anna Christie. So you know him, eh?

MARTHY [*Evasively*]   Seen him about for years.

ANNA   Say, what's he like, tell me, honest?

MARTHY   Oh, he's short and——

ANNA [*Impatiently*]   I don't care what he looks like. What kind is he?

MARTHY [*Earnestly*]   Well, yuh can bet your life, kid, he's as good an old guy as ever walked on two feet. That goes!

ANNA [*Pleased*]   I'm glad to hear it. Then you think he'll stake me to that rest cure I'm after?

MARTHY [*Emphatically*]   Surest thing you know. [*Disgustedly*] But where'd yuh get the idea he was a janitor?

ANNA   He wrote me he was himself.

MARTHY   Well, he was lyin'. He ain't. He's captain of a barge—five men under him.

ANNA [*Disgusted in her turn*]   A barge? What kind of a barge?

MARTHY   Coal, mostly.

ANNA   A coal barge! [*With a harsh laugh*] If that ain't a swell job to find your long lost Old Man working at! Gee, I knew something'd be bound to turn out wrong—always does with me. That puts my idea of his giving me a rest on the bum.

MARTHY   What d'yuh mean?

ANNA   I s'pose he lives on the boat, don't he?

MARTHY   Sure. What about it? Can't you live on it, too?

ANNA [*Scornfully*]   Me? On a dirty coal barge! What d'you think I am?

MARTHY [*Resentfully*]   What d'yuh know about barges, huh? Bet yuh ain't never seen one. That's what comes of his bringing yuh up inland—away from the old devil sea—where yuh'd be safe—Gawd! [*The irony of it strikes her sense of humor and she laughs hoarsely.*]

ANNA [*Angrily*]   His bringing me up! Is that what he tells people! I like his nerve. He let them cousins of my Old Woman keep me on their farm and work me to death like a dog.

MARTHY   Well, he's got queer notions on some things. I've heard him say a farm was the best place for a kid.

ANNA   Sure. That's what he'd always answer back —and a lot of crazy stuff about staying away from the sea—stuff I couldn't make head or tail to. I thought he must be nutty.

MARTHY  He is on that one point. [*Casually*] So yuh didn't fall for life on the farm, huh?

ANNA  I should say not! The old man of the family, his wife, and four sons—I had to slave for all of 'em. I was only a poor relation, and they treated me worse than they dare treat a hired girl. [*After a moment's hesitation—somberly*] It was one of the sons—the youngest—started me—when I was sixteen. After that, I hated 'em so I'd killed 'em all if I'd stayed. So I run away—to St. Paul.

MARTHY [*Who has been listening sympathetically*] I've heard Old Chris talkin' about your bein' a nurse girl out there. Was that all a bluff yuh put up when yuh wrote him?

ANNA  Not on your life, it wasn't. It was true for two years. I didn't go wrong all at one jump. Being a nurse girl was yust what finished me. Taking care of other people's kids, always listening to their bawling and crying, caged in, when you're only a kid yourself and want to go out and see things. At last I got the chance—to get into that house. And you bet your life I took it. [*Defiantly*] And I ain't sorry neither. [*After a pause—with bitter hatred*] It was all men's fault—the whole business. It was men on the farm ordering and beating me—and giving me the wrong start. Then when I was a nurse, it was men again hanging around, bothering me, trying to see what they could get. [*She gives a hard laugh.*] And now it's men all the time. Gawd, I hate 'em, all, every mother's son of 'em! Don't you?

MARTHY  Oh, I dunno. There's good ones and bad ones, kid. You've just had a run of bad luck with 'em, that's all. Your Old Man, now—old Chris—he's a good one.

ANNA [*Sceptically*]  He'll have to show me.

MARTHY  Yuh kept right on writing him yuh was a nurse girl still, even after yuh was in the house, didn't yuh?

ANNA  Sure. [*Cynically*] Not that I think he'd care a darn.

MARTHY  Yuh're all wrong about him, kid. [*Earnestly*] I know Old Chris well for a long time. He's talked to me 'bout you lots o' times. He thinks the world o' you, honest he does.

ANNA  Aw, quit the kiddin'!

MARTHY  Honest! Only, he's a simple old guy, see? He's got nutty notions. But he means well, honest. Listen to me, kid—— [*She is interrupted by the opening and shutting of the street door in the bar and by hearing* CHRIS' *voice.*] Ssshh!

ANNA  What's up?

CHRIS [*Who has entered the bar. He seems considerably sobered up*]  Py golly, Larry, dat grub taste good. Marthy in back?

LARRY  Sure—and another tramp with her. [CHRIS *starts for the entrance to the back room.*]

MARTHY [*To* ANNA *in a hurried, nervous whisper*]  That's him now. He's comin' in here. Brace up!

ANNA  Who? [CHRIS *opens the door.*]

MARTHY [*As if she were greeting him for the first time*]  Why hello, Old Chris. [*Then before he can speak, she shuffles hurriedly past him into the bar, beckoning him to follow her.*] Come here. I wanta tell yuh somethin'. [*He goes out to her. She speaks hurriedly in a low voice.*] Listen! I'm goin' to beat it down to the barge—pack up me duds and blow. That's her in there—your Anna—just come—waitin' for yuh. Treat her right, see? She's been sick. Well, s'long! [*She goes into the back room—to* ANNA.] S'long kid. I gotta beat it now. See yuh later.

ANNA [*Nervously*] So long. [MARTHY *goes quickly out of the family entrance.*]

LARRY [*Looking at the stupefied* CHRIS *curiously*] Well, what's up now?

CHRIS [*Vaguely*] Nutting—nutting. [*He stands before the door to the back room in an agony of embarrassed emotion—then he forces himself to a bold decision, pushes open the door and walks in. He stands there, casts a shy glance at* ANNA, *whose brilliant clothes, and, to him, high-toned appearance, awe him terribly. He looks about him with pitiful nervousness as if to avoid the appraising look with which she takes in his face, his clothes, etc.— his voice seeming to plead for her forbearance.*] Anna!

ANNA [*Acutely embarrassed in her turn*] Hello —Father. She told me it was you. I yust got here a little while ago.

CHRIS [*Goes slowly over to her chair*] It's good —for see you—after all dem years, Anna. [*He bends down over her. After an embarrassed struggle they manage to kiss each other.*]

ANNA [*A trace of genuine feeling in her voice*] It's good to see you, too.

CHRIS [*Grasps her arms and looks into her face—then overcome by a wave of fierce tenderness*] Anna lilla! Anna lilla! [*Takes her in his arms.*]

ANNA [*Shrinks away from him, half-frightened*] What's that—Swedish? I don't know it. [*Then as if seeking relief from the tension in a voluble chatter*] Gee, I had an awful trip coming here. I'm all in. I had to sit up in the dirty coach all night—couldn't get no sleep, hardly—and then I had a hard job finding this place. I never been in New York before, you know, and——

CHRIS [*Who has been staring down at her face admiringly, not hearing what she says—impulsively*] You know you vas awful pooty gel, Anna? Ay bet all men see you fall in love with you, py yiminy!

ANNA [*Repelled—harshly*] Cut it! You talk same as they all do.

CHRIS [*Hurt—humbly*] Ain't no harm for your fader talk dat vay, Anna.

ANNA [*Forcing a short laugh*] No—course not. Only—it's funny to see you and not remember nothing. You're like—a stranger.

CHRIS [*Sadly*] Ay s'pose. Ay never come home only few times ven you vas kit in Sveden. You don't remember dat?

ANNA No. [*Resentfully*] But why didn't you never come home them days? Why didn't you never come out West to see me?

CHRIS [*Slowly*] Ay tank, after your mo'der die, ven Ay vas avay on voyage, it's better for you you don't never see me! [*He sinks down in the chair opposite her dejectedly—then turns to her—sadly.*] Ay don't know, Anna, vhy Ay never come home Sveden in old year. Ay vant come home end of every voyage. Ay vant see your mo'der, your two bro'der before dey vas drowned, you ven you vas born—but—Ay—don't go. Ay sign on oder ships—go South America, go Australia, go China, go every port all over world many times—but Ay never go aboard ship sail for Sveden. Ven Ay gat money for pay passage home as passenger den—— [*He bows his head guiltily.*] Ay forgat and Ay spend all money. Ven Ay tank again, it's too late. [*He sighs.*] Ay don't know why but dat's vay with most sailor fallar, Anna. Dat ole davil sea make dem crazy fools with her dirty tricks. It's so.

ANNA [*Who has watched him keenly while he has been speaking—with a trace of scorn in her voice*] Then you think the sea's to blame for everything, eh? Well, you're still workin' on it, ain't you, spite of all you used to write me about hating it. That dame was here told me you was captain of a coal barge—and you wrote me you was yanitor of a building!

CHRIS [*Embarrassed but lying glibly*] Oh, Ay work on land long time as yanitor. Yust short time ago Ay got dis yob cause Ay vas sick, need open air.

ANNA [*Sceptically*] Sick? You? You'd never think it.

CHRIS And, Anna, dis ain't real sailor yob. Dis ain't real boat on sea. She's yust old tub—like piece of land with house on it dat float. Yob on her ain't sea yob. No. Ay don't gat yob on sea, Anna, if Ay die first. Ay swear dat ven your mo'der die. Ay keep my word, py yingo!

ANNA [*Perplexed*] Well, I can't see no difference. [*Dismissing the subject*] Speaking of being sick, I been there myself—yust out of the hospital two weeks ago.

CHRIS [*Immediately all concern*] You, Anna? Py golly! [*Anxiously*] You feel better now, dough, don't you? You look little tired dat's all!

ANNA [*Wearily*] I am. Tired to death. I need a long rest and I don't see much chance of getting it.

CHRIS What do you mean, Anna?

ANNA Well, when I made up my mind to come to see you, I thought you was a yanitor—that you'd have a place where, maybe, if you didn't mind having me, I could visit a while and rest up—till I felt able to get back on the job again.

CHRIS [*Eagerly*] But Ay gat place, Anna—nice place. You rest all you want, py yiminy! You don't never have to vork as nurse gel no more. You stay with me, py golly!

ANNA [*Surprised and pleased by his eagerness—with a smile*] Then you're really glad to see me—honest?

CHRIS [*Pressing one of her hands in both of his*] Anna, Ay like see you like hell, Ay tal you! And don't you talk no more about gatting yob. You stay with me. Ay don't see you for long time, you don't forgat dat. [*His voice trembles.*] Ay'm gatting ole. Ay gat no one in vorld but you.

ANNA [*Touched—embarrassed by this unfamiliar emotion*] Thanks. It sounds good to hear someone —talk to me that way. Say, though—if you're so lonely—it's funny—why ain't you ever married again?

CHRIS [*Shaking his head emphatically—after a pause*] Ay love your mo'der too much for ever do dat, Anna.

ANNA [*Impressed—slowly*] I don't remember nothing about her. What was she like? Tell me.

CHRIS Ay tal you all about everytang—and you tal me all tangs happen to you. But not here now. Dis ain't good place for young gel, anyway. Only no good sailor fallar come here for gat drunk. [*He gets to his feet quickly and picks up her bag.*] You come with me, Anna. You need lie down, gat rest.

ANNA [*Half rises to her feet, then sits down again*] Where're you going?

CHRIS Come. Ve gat on board.

ANNA [*Disappointedly*] On board your barge, you mean? [*Dryly*] Nix for mine! [*Then seeing his crestfallen look—forcing a smile*] Do you think that's a good place for a young girl like me—a coal barge?

CHRIS [*Dully*] Yes, Ay tank. [*He hesitates—then continues more and more pleadingly*] You don't know how nice it's on barge, Anna. Tug come and ve gat towed out on voyage—yust water all round, and sun, and fresh air, and good grub for make you strong, healthy gel. You see many tangs you don't see before. You gat moonlight at night, maybe; see steamer pass; see schooner make sail—see everytang dat's pooty. You need take rest like dat. You work too hard for young gel already. You need vacation, yes!

ANNA [*Who has listened to him with a growing*

*interest—with an uncertain laugh*] It sounds good to hear you tell it. I'd sure like a trip on the water, all right. It's the barge idea has me stopped. Well, I'll go down with you and have a look—and maybe I'll take a chance. Gee, I'd do anything once.

CHRIS [*Picks up her bag again*] Ve go, eh?

ANNA What's the rush? Wait a second. [*Forgetting the situation for a moment, she relapses into the familiar form and flashes one of her winning trade smiles at him.*] Gee, I'm thirsty.

CHRIS [*Sets down her bag immediately—hastily*] Ay'm sorry, Anna. What you tank you like for drink, eh?

ANNA [*Promptly*] I'll take a—— [*Then suddenly reminded—confusedly*] I don't know. What'a they got here?

CHRIS [*With a grin*] Ay don't tank dey got much fancy drink for young gel in dis place, Anna. Yinger ale—sas-prilla, maybe.

ANNA [*Forcing a laugh herself*] Make it sas, then.

CHRIS [*Coming up to her—with a wink*] Ay tal you, Anna, ve calabrate, yes—dis one time because ve meet after many year. [*In a half whisper, embarrassedly.*] Dey gat good port-wine, Anna. It's good for you, Ay tank—little bit—for give you appetite. It ain't strong, neider. One glass don't go to your head, Ay promise.

ANNA [*With a half hysterical laugh*] All right. I'll take port.

CHRIS Ay go gat him. [*He goes to the bar. As soon as the door closes,* ANNA *starts to her feet.*]

ANNA [*Picking up her bag—half-aloud—stammeringly*] Gawd, I can't stand this! I better beat it. [*Then she lets her bag drop, stumbles over to her chair again, and covering her face with her hands, begins to sob.*]

LARRY [*Putting down his paper as* CHRIS *comes up—with a grin*] Well, who's the blonde?

CHRIS [*Proudly*] Dat vas Anna, Larry.

LARRY [*In amazement*] Your daughter, Anna? [CHRIS *nods.* LARRY *lets a long, low whistle escape him and turns away embarrassedly.*]

CHRIS Don't you tank she vas pooty gel, Larry?

LARRY [*Rising to the occasion*] Sure! A peach!

CHRIS You bet you! Give me drink for take back—one port vine for Anna—she calabrate dis one time with me—and small beer for me.

LARRY [*As he gets the drinks*] Small beer for you, eh? She's reformin' you already.

CHRIS [*Pleased*] You bet! [*He takes the drinks. As she hears him coming,* ANNA *hastily dries her eyes, tries to smile.* CHRIS *comes in and sets the drinks down on the table—stares at her for a second anxiously—patting her hand.*] You look tired, Anna. Vell, Ay make you take good long rest now. [*Picking up his beer*] Come, you drink vine. It puts new life in you. [*She lifts her glass—he grins.*] Skoal, Anna! You know dat Svedish word?

ANNA Skoal! [*Downing her port at a gulp like a drink of whisky—her lips trembling*] Skoal? Guess I know that word, all right!

[*The curtain falls.*]

# ACT TWO

SCENE *Ten days later. The stern of the deeply-laden barge, Simeon Winthrop, at anchor in the outer harbor of Provincetown, Mass. It is ten o'clock at night. Dense fog shrouds the barge on all sides, and she floats motionless on a calm. A lantern set up on an immense coil of thick hawser sheds a dull, filtering light on objects near it—the heavy steel bits for making fast the tow lines, etc. In the rear is the cabin, its misty windows glowing wanly with the light of a lamp inside. The chimney of the cabin stove rises a few feet above the roof. The doleful tolling of bells, on Long Point, on ships at anchor, breaks the silence at regular intervals.*

*As the curtain rises,* ANNA *is discovered standing near the coil of rope on which the lantern is placed. She looks healthy, transformed, the natural color has come back to her face. She has on a black oilskin coat, but wears no hat. She is staring out into the fog astern with an expression of awed wonder.*

*The cabin door is pushed open and* CHRIS *appears. He is dressed in yellow oilskins—coat, pants, sou'wester—and wears high sea-boots.*

CHRIS [*The glare from the cabin still in his eyes, peers blinkingly astern*] Anna! [*Receiving no reply, he calls again, this time with apparent apprehension.*] Anna!

ANNA [*With a start—making a gesture with her hand as if to impose silence—in a hushed whisper*] Yes, here I am. What d'you want?

CHRIS [*Walks over to her—solicitously*] Don't you come turn in, Anna? It's late—after four bells. It ain't good for you stay out here in fog, Ay tank.

ANNA Why not? [*With a trace of strange exultation*] I love this fog! Honest! It's so—— [*She hesitates, groping for a word*] Funny and still. I feel as if I was—out of things altogether.

CHRIS [*Spitting disgustedly*] Fog's vorst one of her dirty tricks, py yingo!

ANNA [*With a short laugh*] Beefing about the sea again? I'm getting so's I love it, the little I've seen.

CHRIS [*Glancing at her moodily*] Dat's foolish talk, Anna. You see her more, you don't talk dat vay. [*Then seeing her irritation, he hastily adopts a more cheerful tone.*] But Ay'm glad you like it on barge. Ay'm glad it makes you feel good again. [*With a placating grin*] You like live like dis alone with ol fa'der, eh?

ANNA Sure I do. Everything's been so different from anything I ever come across before. And now

—this fog—— Gee, I wouldn't have missed it for nothing. I never thought living on ships was so different from land. Gee, I'd yust love to work on it, honest I would, if I was a man. I don't wonder you always been a sailor.

CHRIS [*Vehemently*] Ay ain't sailor, Anna. And dis ain't real sea. You only see nice part. [*Then as she doesn't answer, he continues hopefully*] Vell, fog lift in morning, Ay tank.

ANNA [*The exultation again in her voice*] I love it! I don't give a rap if it never lifts! [CHRIS *fidgets from one foot to the other worriedly.* ANNA *continues slowly, after a pause*] It makes me feel clean —out here—'s if I'd taken a bath.

CHRIS [*After a pause*] You better go in cabin read book. Dat put you to sleep.

ANNA I don't want to sleep. I want to stay out here—and think about things.

CHRIS [*Walks away from her toward the cabin— then comes back*] You act funny tonight, Anna.

ANNA [*Her voice rising angrily*] Say, what're you trying to do—make things rotten? You been kind as kind can be to me and I certainly appreciate it—only don't spoil it all now. [*Then, seeing the hurt expression on her father's face, she forces a smile.*] Let's talk of something else. Come. Sit down here. [*She points to the coil of rope.*]

CHRIS [*Sits down beside her with a sigh*] It's gatting pooty late in night, Anna. Must be near five bells.

ANNA [*Interestedly*] Five bells? What time is that?

CHRIS  Half past ten.

ANNA  Funny I don't know nothing about sea talk—but those cousins was always talking crops and that stuff. Gee, wasn't I sick of it—and of them!

CHRIS  You don't like live on farm, Anna?

ANNA  I've told you a hundred times I hated it. [*Decidedly*] I'd rather have one drop of ocean than all the farms in the world! Honest! And you wouldn't like a farm, neither. Here's where you belong. [*She makes a sweeping gesture seaward.*] But not on a coal barge. You belong on a real ship, sailing all over the world.

CHRIS  [*Moodily*] Ay've done dat many year, Anna, when Ay vas damn fool.

ANNA  [*Disgustedly*] Oh, rats! [*After a pause she speaks musingly.*] Was the men in our family always sailors—as far back as you know about?

CHRIS  [*Shortly*] Yes. Damn fools! All men in our village on coast, Sveden, go to sea. Ain't nutting else for dem to do. My fa'der die on board ship in Indian Ocean. He's buried at sea. Ay don't never know him only little bit. Den my tree bro'der, older'n me, dey go on ships. Den Ay go, too. Den my mo'der she's left all 'lone. She die pooty quick after dat—all 'lone. Ve vas all avay on voyage when she die. [*He pauses sadly.*] Two my bro'der dey gat lost on fishing boat same like your bro'ders vas drowned. My oder bro'der, he save money, give up sea, den he die home in bed. He's only one dat ole davil don't kill. [*Defiantly*] But me, Ay bet you Ay die ashore in bed, too!

ANNA  Were all of 'em just plain sailors?

CHRIS  Able body seaman, most of dem. [*With a certain pride*] Dey vas all smart seaman, too—A one. [*Then after hesitating a moment—shyly*] Ay vas bosun.

ANNA  Bosun?

CHRIS  Dat's kind of officer.

ANNA  Gee, that was fine. What does he do?

CHRIS [*After a second's hesitation, plunged into gloom again by his fear of her enthusiasm*] Hard vork all time. It's rotten. Ay tal you, for go to sea. [*Determined to disgust her with sea life—volubly*] Dey're all fool fallar, dem fallar in our family. Dey all vork rotten yob on sea for nutting, don't care nutting but yust gat big pay day in pocket, gat drunk, gat robbed, ship avay again on oder voyage. Dey don't come home. Dey don't do anytang like good man do. And dat ole davil, sea, sooner, later she svallow dem up.

ANNA [*With an excited laugh*] Good sports, I'd call 'em. [*Then hastily*] But say—listen—did all the women of the family marry sailors?

CHRIS [*Eagerly—seeing a chance to drive home his point*] Yes—and it's bad on dem like hell vorst of all. Dey don't see deir men only once in long while. Dey set and vait all 'lone. And vhen deir boys grows up, go to sea, dey sit and vait some more. [*Vehemently*] Any gel marry sailor, she's crazy fool! Your mo'der she tal you same tang if she vas alive. [*He relapses into an attitude of somber brooding.*]

ANNA [*After a pause—dreamily*] Funny! I do feel sort of—nutty, tonight. I feel old.

CHRIS [*Mystified*]  Ole?

ANNA  Sure—like I'd been living a long, long time—out here in the fog. [*Frowning perplexedly*] I don't know how to tell you yust what I mean. It's like I'd come home after a long visit away some place. It all seems like I'd been here before lots of times—on boats—in this same fog. [*With a short laugh*] You must think I'm off my base.

CHRIS [*Gruffly*]  Anybody feel funny dat vay in fog.

ANNA [*Persistently*]  But why d'you s'pose I feel so—so—like I'd found something I'd missed and been looking for— 's if this was the right place for me to fit in? And I seem to have forgot—everything that's happened—like it didn't matter no more. And I feel clean, somehow—like you feel yust after you've took a bath. And I feel happy for once—yes, honest! —happier than I ever have been anywhere before! [*As* CHRIS *makes no comment but a heavy sigh, she continues wonderingly.*] It's nutty for me to feel that way, don't you think?

CHRIS [*A grim foreboding in his voice*]  Ay tank Ay'm damn fool for bring you on voyage, Anna.

ANNA [*Impressed by his tone*]  You talk nutty tonight yourself. You act 's if you was scared something was going to happen.

CHRIS  Only God know dat, Anna.

ANNA [*Half-mockingly*]  Then it'll be Gawd's will, like the preachers say—what does happen.

CHRIS [*Starts to his feet with fierce protest*]  No! Dat ole davil, sea, she ain't God! [*In the pause of silence that comes after his defiance a hail in a man's husky, exhausted voice comes faintly out of the fog to port*] Ahoy! [CHRIS *gives a startled exclamation.*]

ANNA [*Jumping to her feet*]   What's that?

CHRIS [*Who has regained his composure—sheepishly*]   Py golly, dat scare me for minute. It's only some fallar hail, Anna—loose his course in fog. Must be fisherman's power boat. His engine break down, Ay guess. [*The "ahoy" comes again through the wall of fog, sounding much nearer this time.* CHRIS *goes over to the port bulwark.*] Sound from dis side. She come in from open sea. [*He holds his hands to his mouth, megaphone-fashion, and shouts back.*] Ahoy, dere! Vhat's trouble?

THE VOICE [*This time sounding nearer but up forward toward the bow*]   Heave a rope when we come alongside. [*Then irritably*] Where are ye, ye scut?

CHRIS   Ay hear dem rowing. Dey come up by bow, Ay tank. [*Then shouting out again*] Dis vay!

THE VOICE   Right ye are! [*There is a muffled sound of oars in oar-locks.*]

ANNA [*Half to herself—resentfully*]   Why don't that guy stay where he belongs?

CHRIS [*Hurriedly*]   Ay go up bow. All hands asleep 'cepting fallar on vatch. Ay gat heave line to dat fallar. [*He picks up a coil of rope and hurries off toward the bow.* ANNA *walks back toward the extreme stern as if she wanted to remain as much isolated as possible. She turns her back on the proceedings and stares out into the fog.* THE VOICE *is heard again shouting "Ahoy" and* CHRIS *answering "Dis vay." Then there is a pause—the murmur of excited voices—then the scuffling of feet.* CHRIS *appears from around the cabin to port. He is supporting the limp form of a man dressed in dungarees, holding one of the man's arms around his neck. The deckhand,* JOHNSON, *a young blond Swede, follows him, helping along another exhausted man similar fashion.* ANNA *turns to look at them.* CHRIS *stops for a second—volubly.*] Anna! You come help, vill you? You find vhisky in cabin. Dese fallars need drink for fix dem. Dey vas near dead.

ANNA [*Hurrying to him*] Sure—but who are they? What's the trouble?

CHRIS Sailor fallars. Deir steamer gat wrecked. Dey been five days in open boat—four fallars—only one left able stand up. Come, Anna. [*She precedes him into the cabin, holding the door open while he and* JOHNSON *carry in their burdens. The door is shut, then opened again as* JOHNSON *comes out.* CHRIS' *voice shouts after him.*] Go gat oder fallar, Yohnson.

JOHNSON Yes, sir. [*He goes. The door is closed again.* MAT BURKE *stumbles in around the port side of the cabin. He moves slowly, feeling his way uncertainly, keeping hold of the port bulwark with his right hand to steady himself. He is stripped to the waist, has on nothing but a pair of dirty dungaree pants. He is a powerful, broad-chested six-footer, his face handsome in a hard, rough, bold, defiant way. He is about thirty, in the full power of his heavy-muscled, immense strength. His dark eyes are bloodshot and wild for sleeplessness. The muscles of his arms and shoulders are lumped in knots and bunches, the veins of his fore-arms stand out like blue cords. He finds his way to the coil of hawser and sits down on it facing the cabin, his back bowed, head in hands, in an attitude of spent weariness.*]

BURKE [*Talking aloud to himself*] Row, ye divil! Row! [*Then lifting his head and looking about him.*] What's this tub? Well, we're safe anyway—with the help of God. [*He makes the sign of the cross mechanically.* JOHNSON *comes along the deck to port, supporting the fourth man, who is babbling to himself incoherently.* BURKE *glances at him disdainfully.*] Is it losing the small wits ye iver had, ye are? Deck-scrubbing scut! [*They pass him and go into the cabin, leaving the door open.* BURKE *sags forward wearily.*] I'm bate out—bate out entirely.

ANNA [*Comes out of the cabin with a tumbler quarter-full of whisky in her hand. She gives a start when she sees* BURKE *so near her, the light from the open door falling full on him. Then, overcoming what is evidently a feeling of repulsion, she comes up beside him.*] Here you are. Here's a drink for you. You need it, I guess.

BURKE [*Lifting his head slowly—confusedly*]. It is dreaming I am?

ANNA [*Half smiling*] Drink it and you'll find it ain't no dream.

BURKE To hell with the drink—but I'll take it just the same. [*He tosses it down.*] Ahah! I'm needin' that—and 'tis fine stuff. [*Looking up at her with frank, grinning admiration.*] But 'twasn't the booze I meant when I said, was I dreaming. I thought you was some mermaid out of the sea come to torment me. [*He reaches out to feel of her arm.*] Aye, rale flesh and blood, divil a less.

ANNA [*Coldly. Stepping back from him*] Cut that.

BURKE But tell me, isn't this a barge I'm on—or isn't it?

ANNA Sure.

BURKE And what is a fine handsome woman the like of you doing on this scow?

ANNA [*Coldly*] Never you mind. [*Then half-amused in spite of herself.*] Say, you're a great one, honest—starting right in kidding after what you been through.

BURKE [*Delighted—proudly*] Ah, it was nothing —aisy for a rale man with guts to him, the like of me. [*He laughs.*] All in the day's work, darlin'. [*Then, more seriously but still in a boastful tone, confidentially*] But I won't be denying 'twas a damn narrow squeak. We'd all ought to be with Davy Jones at the bottom of the sea, be rights. And only for me, I'm telling you, and the great strength and guts is in me, we'd be being scoffed by the fishes this minute!

ANNA [*Contemptuously*] Gee, you hate yourself, don't you? [*Then turning away from him indifferently*] Well, you'd better come in and lie down. You must want to sleep.

BURKE [*Stung—rising unsteadily to his feet with chest out and head thrown back—resentfully*] Lie down and sleep, is it? Divil a wink I'm after having for two days and nights and divil a bit I'm needing now. Let you not be thinking I'm the like of them three weak scuts come in the boat with me. I could lick the three of them sitting down with one hand tied behind me. They may be bate out, but I'm not—and I've been rowing the boat with them lying in the bottom not able to raise a hand for the last two days we was in it. [*Furiously, as he sees this is making no impression on her*] And I can lick all hands on this tub, wan be wan, tired as I am!

ANNA [*Sarcastically*] Gee, ain't you a hard guy! [*Then, with a trace of sympathy, as she notices him swaying from weakness*] But never mind that fight talk. I'll take your word for all you've said. Go on and sit down out here, anyway, if I can't get you to come inside. [*He sits down weakly.*] You're all in, you might as well own up to it.

BURKE [*Fiercely*] The hell I am!

ANNA [*Coldly*] Well, be stubborn then for all I care. And I must say I don't care for your language. The men I know don't pull that rough stuff when ladies are around.

BURKE [*Getting unsteadily to his feet again—in a rage*] Ladies! Ho-ho! Divil mend you! Let you not be making game of me. What would ladies be doing on this bloody hulk? [*As* ANNA *attempts to go to the cabin, he lurches into her path.*] Aisy, now! You're not the old Squarehead's woman, I suppose you'll be telling me next—living in his cabin with him, no less! [*Seeing the cold, hostile expression on* ANNA'S *face, he suddenly changes his tone to one of boisterous joviality*] But I do be thinking, iver since the first look my eyes took at you, that it's a fool you are to be wasting yourself—a fine, handsome girl—on a stumpy runt of a man like that old Swede. There's too many strapping great lads on the sea would give their heart's blood for one kiss of you!

ANNA [*Scornfully*] Lads like you, eh?

BURKE [*Grinning*] Ye take the words out o' my mouth. I'm the proper lad for you, if it's meself do be saying it. [*With a quick movement he puts his arms about her waist.*] Whisht, now, me daisy! Himself's in the cabin. It's wan of your kisses I'm needing to take the tiredness from me bones. Wan kiss, now! [*He presses her to him and attempts to kiss her.*]

ANNA [*Struggling fiercely*] Leggo of me, you big mutt! [*She pushes him away with all her might. BURKE, weak and tottering, is caught off his guard. He is thrown down backward and, in falling, hits his head a hard thump against the bulwark. He lies there still, knocked out for the moment. ANNA, stands for a second, looking down at him frightenedly. Then she kneels down beside him and raises his head to her knee, staring into his face anxiously for some sign of life.*]

BURKE [*Stirring a bit—mutteringly*] God stiffen it! [*He opens his eyes and blinks up at her with vague wonder.*]

ANNA [*Letting his head sink back on the deck, rising to her feet with a sigh of relief*] You're coming to all right, eh? Gee, I was scared for a moment I'd killed you.

BURKE [*With difficulty rising to a sitting position—scornfully*] Killed, is it? It'd take more than a bit of a blow to crack my thick skull. [*Then looking at *her with the most intense admiration*] But, glory be, it's a power of strength is in them two fine arms of yours. There's not a man in the world can say the same as you, that he seen Mat Burke lying at his feet and him dead to the world.

ANNA [*Rather remorsefully*] Forget it. I'm sorry it happened, see? [*Burke rises and sits on bench. Then severely*] Only you had no right to be getting fresh with me. Listen, now, and don't go getting any more wrong notions. I'm on this barge because I'm making a trip with my father. The captain's my father. Now you know.

BURKE  The old square—the old Swede, I mean?

ANNA  Yes.

BURKE [*Rising—peering at her face*] Sure I might have known it, if I wasn't a bloody fool from birth. Where else'd you get that fine yellow hair is like a golden crown on your head.

ANNA [*With an amused laugh*] Say, nothing stops you, does it? [*Then attempting a severe tone again*] But don't you think you ought to be apologizing for what you said and done yust a minute ago, instead of trying to kid me with that mush?

BURKE [*Indignantly*] Mush! [*Then bending forward toward her with very intense earnestness*] Indade and I will ask your pardon a thousand times—and on my knees, if ye like. I didn't mean a word of what I said or did. [*Resentful again for a second*] But divil a woman in all the ports of the world has iver made a great fool of me that way before!

ANNA [*With amused sarcasm*]  I see. You mean you're a lady-killer and they all fall for you.

BURKE [*Offended. Passionately*] Leave off your fooling! 'Tis that is after getting my back up at you. [*Earnestly*] 'Tis no lie I'm telling you about the women. [*Ruefully*] Though it's a great jackass I am to be mistaking you, even in anger, for the like of them cows on the waterfront is the only women I've met up with since I was growed to a man. [*As* ANNA *shrinks away from him at this, he hurries on pleadingly*] I'm a hard, rough man and I'm not fit, I'm thinking, to be kissing the shoe-soles of a fine, decent girl the like of yourself. 'Tis only the ignorance of your kind made me see you wrong. So you'll forgive me, for the love of God, and let us be friends from this out. [*Passionately*] I'm thinking I'd rather be friends with you than have my wish for anything else in the world. [*He holds out his hand to her shyly.*]

ANNA [*Looking queerly at him, perplexed and worried, but moved and pleased in spite of herself—takes his hand uncertainly*] Sure.

BURKE [*With boyish delight*] God bless you! [*In his excitement he squeezes her hand tight.*]

ANNA Ouch!

BURKE [*Hastily dropping her hand—ruefully*] Your pardon, Miss. 'Tis a clumsy ape I am. [*Then simply—glancing down his arm proudly.*] It's great power I have in my hand and arm, and I do be forgetting it at times.

ANNA [*Nursing her crushed hand and glancing at his arm, not without a trace of his own admiration*] Gee, you're some strong, all right.

BURKE [*Delighted*] It's no lie, and why shouldn't

I be, with me shoveling a million tons of coal in the stokeholes of ships since I was a lad only. [*He pats the coil of hawser invitingly.*] Let you sit down, now, Miss, and I'll be telling you a bit of myself, and you'll be telling me a bit of yourself, and in an hour we'll be as old friends as if we was born in the same house. [*He pulls at her sleeve shyly.*] Sit down now, if you plaze.

ANNA [*With a half laugh*] Well—— [*She sits down.*] But we won't talk about me, see? You tell me about yourself and about the wreck.

BURKE [*Flattered*] I'll tell you, surely. But can I be asking you one question, Miss, has my head in a puzzle?

ANNA [*Guardedly*] Well—I dunno—what is it?

BURKE What is it you do when you're not taking a trip with the Old Man? For I'm thinking a fine girl the like of you ain't living always on this tub.

ANNA [*Uneasily*] No—of course I ain't. [*She searches his face suspiciously, afraid there may be some hidden insinuation in his words. Seeing his simple frankness, she goes on confidently.*] Well, I'll tell you. I'm a governess, see? I take care of kids for people and learn them things.

BURKE [*Impressed*] A governess, is it? You must be smart, surely.

ANNA Let's not talk about me. Tell me about the wreck, like you promised me you would.

BURKE [*Importantly*] 'Twas this way, Miss. Two weeks out we ran into the divil's own storm, and she sprang wan hell of a leak up for'ard. The skipper was hoping to make Boston before another blow would finish her, but ten days back we met up with another storm the like of the first, only worse. Four days we was in it with green seas raking over her from bow to stern. That was a terrible time, God help us. [*Proudly*] And if 'twasn't for me and my great strength, I'm telling you—and it's God's truth —there'd been mutiny itself in the stokehole. 'Twas me held them to it, with a kick to wan and a clout to another, and they not caring a damn for the engineers any more, but fearing a clout of my right arm more than they'd fear the sea itself. [*He glances at her anxiously, eager for her approval.*]

ANNA [*Concealing a smile—amused by this boyish boasting of his*] You did some hard work, didn't you?

BURKE [*Promptly*] I did that! I'm a divil for sticking it out when them that's weak give up. But much good it did anyone! 'Twas a mad, fightin' scramble in the last seconds with each man for himself. I disremember how it come about, but there was the four of us in wan boat and when we raised high on a great wave I took a look about and divil a sight there was of ship or men on top of the sea.

ANNA [*In a subdued voice*] Then all the others was drowned?

BURKE They was, surely.

ANNA [*With a shudder*] What a terrible end!

BURKE [*Turns to her*] A terrible end for the like of them swabs does live on land, maybe. But for the like of us does be roaming the seas, a good end, I'm telling you—quick and clane.

ANNA [*Struck by the word*] Yes, clean. That's

yust the word for—all of it—the way it makes me feel.

BURKE  The sea, you mean? [*Interestedly*] I'm thinking you have a bit of it in your blood, too. Your Old Man wasn't only a barge rat—begging your pardon—all his life, by the cut of him.

ANNA  No, he was bosun on sailing ships for years. And all the men on both sides of the family have gone to sea as far back as he remembers, he says. All the women have married sailors, too.

BURKE  [*With intense satisfaction*] Did they, now? They had spirit in them. It's only on the sea you'd find rale men with guts is fit to wed with fine, high-tempered girls [*then he adds half-boldly*] the like of yourself.

ANNA  [*With a laugh*] There you go kiddin' again. [*Then seeing his hurt expression—quickly*] But you was going to tell be about yourself. You're Irish, of course I can tell that.

BURKE  [*Stoutly*]  Yes, thank God, though I've not seen a sight of it in fifteen years or more.

ANNA  [*Thoughtfully*]  Sailors never do go home hardly, do they? That's what my father was saying.

BURKE  He wasn't telling no lie. [*With sudden melancholy*] It's a hard and lonesome life, the sea is. The only women you'd meet in the ports of the world who'd be willing to speak you a kind word isn't a woman at all. You know the kind I mane, and they're a poor, wicked lot, God forgive them. They're looking to steal the money from you only.

ANNA  [*Her face averted—rising to her feet—agitatedly*]  I think—I guess I'd better see what's doing inside.

ANNA CHRISTIE 105

BURKE [*Afraid he has offended her—beseechingly*] Don't go, I'm saying! Is it I've given you offense with the talk of the like of them? Don't heed it at all! I'm clumsy in my wits when it comes to talking proper with a girl the like of you. And why wouldn't I be? Since the day I left home for to go to sea punching coal, this is the first time I've had a word with a rale, dacent woman. So don't turn your back on me now, and we beginning to be friends.

ANNA [*Turning to him again—forcing a smile*] I'm not sore at you, honest.

BURKE [*Gratefully*] God bless you!

ANNA [*Changing the subject abruptly*] But if you honestly think the sea's such a rotten life, why don't you get out of it?

BURKE [*Surprised*] Work on land, is it? [*She nods. He spits scornfully.*] Digging spuds in the muck from dawn to dark, I suppose? [*Vehemently*] I wasn't made for it, Miss.

ANNA [*With a laugh*] I thought you'd say that.

BURKE [*Argumentatively*] But there's good jobs and bad jobs at sea, like there'd be on land. I'm thinking if it's in the stokehole of a proper liner I was, I'd be able to have a little house and be home to it wan week out of four. And I'm thinking that maybe then I'd have the luck to find a fine dacent girl—the like of yourself, now—would be willing to wed with me.

ANNA [*Turning away from him with a short laugh—uneasily*] Why, sure. Why not?

BURKE [*Edging up close to her—exultantly*] Then you think a girl the like of yourself might maybe not mind the past at all but only be seeing the good herself put in me?

ANNA [*In the same tone*] Why, sure.

BURKE [*Passionately*] She'd not be sorry for it, I'd take my oath! 'Tis no more drinking and roving about I'd be doing then, but giving my pay day into her hand and staying at home with her as meek as a lamb each night of the week I'd be in port.

ANNA [*Moved in spite of herself and troubled by this half-concealed proposal—with a forced laugh*] All you got to do is find the girl.

BURKE I have found her!

ANNA [*Half-frightenedly—trying to laugh it off*] You have? When? I thought you was saying——

BURKE [*Boldly and forcefully*] This night. [*Hanging his head—humbly*] If she'll be having me. [*Then raising his eyes to hers—simply*] 'Tis you I mean.

ANNA [*Is held by his eyes for a moment—then shrinks back from him with a strange, broken laugh*] Say—are you—going crazy? Are you trying to kid me? Proposing—to me!—for Gawd's sake!—on such short acquaintance? [CHRIS *comes out of the cabin and stands staring blinkingly astern. When he makes out* ANNA *in such intimate proximity to this strange sailor, an angry expression comes over his face.*]

BURKE [*Following her—with fierce, pleading insistence*] I'm telling you there's the will of God in it that brought me safe through the storm and fog to the wan spot in the world where you was! Think of that now, and isn't it queer——

CHRIS Anna! [*He comes toward them, raging, his fists clenched.*] Anna, you gat in cabin, you hear!

ANNA [*All her emotions immediately transformed into resentment at his bullying tone*] Who d'you think you're talking to—a slave?

CHRIS [*Hurt—his voice breaking—pleadingly*] You need gat rest, Anna. You gat sleep. [*She does not move. He turns on* BURKE *furiously.*] What you doing here, you sailor fallar? You ain't sick like oders. You gat in fo'c's'le. Dey give you bunk. [*Threateningly*] You hurry. Ay tal you!

ANNA [*Impulsively*] But he is sick. Look at him. Look at him. He can hardly stand up.

BURKE [*Straightening and throwing out his chest —with a bold laugh*] Is it giving me orders ye are, me bucko? Let you look out, then! With wan hand, weak as I am, I can break ye in two and fling the pieces over the side—and your crew after you. [*Stopping abruptly*] I was forgetting. You're her Old Man and I'd not raise a fist to you for the world. [*His knees sag, he wavers and seems about to fall.* ANNA *utters an exclamation of alarm and hurries to his side.*]

ANNA [*Taking one of his arms over her shoulder*] Come on in the cabin. You can have my bed if there ain't no other place.

BURKE [*With jubilant happiness—as they proceed toward the cabin*] Glory be to God, is it holding my arm about your neck you are! Anna! Anna! Sure it's a sweet name is suited to you.

ANNA [*Guiding him carefully*] Sssh! Sssh!

BURKE  Whisht, is it? Indade, and I'll not. I'll be roaring it out like a fog horn over the sea! You're the girl of the world and we'll be marrying soon and I don't care who knows it!

ANNA [*As she guides him through the cabin door*] Ssshh! Never mind that talk. You go to sleep. [*They go out of sight in the cabin.* CHRIS, *who has been listening to* BURKE's *last words with open-mouthed amazement, stands looking after them desperately.*]

CHRIS [*Turns suddenly and shakes his fist out at the sea—with bitter hatred*]  Dat's your dirty trick, damn ole davil, you! [*Then in a frenzy of rage*] But, py God, you don't do dat! Not vhile Ay'm living! No, py God, you don't!

[*The curtain falls.*]

# ACT THREE

SCENE *The interior of the cabin on the barge, Simeon Winthrop (at dock in Boston)—a narrow, low-ceilinged compartment the walls of which are painted a light brown with white trimmings. In the rear on the left, a door leading to the sleeping quarters. In the far left corner, a large locker-closet, painted white, on the door of which a mirror hangs on a nail. In the rear wall, two small square windows and a door opening out on the deck toward the stern. In the right wall, two more windows looking out on the port deck. White curtains, clean and stiff, are at the windows. A table with two cane-bottomed chairs stands in the center of the cabin. A dilapidated, wicker rocker, painted brown, is also by the table.*

*It is afternoon of a sunny day about a week later. From the harbor and docks outside, muffled by the closed door and windows, comes the sound of steamers' whistles and the*

*puffing snort of the donkey engines of some
ship unloading nearby.*

*As the curtain rises,* CHRIS *and* ANNA *are
discovered.* ANNA *is seated in the rocking-
chair by the table, with a newspaper in her
hands. She is not reading but staring straight
in front of her. She looks unhappy, troubled,
frowningly concentrated on her thoughts.*
CHRIS *wanders about the room, casting quick,
uneasy side glances at her face, then stopping
to peer absent-mindedly out of the window.
His attitude betrays an overwhelming,
gloomy anxiety which has him on tenter-
hooks. He pretends to be engaged in setting
things ship-shape, but this occupation is con-
fined to picking up some object, staring at it
stupidly for a second, then aimlessly putting
it down again. He clears his throat and starts
to sing to himself in a low, doleful voice:* "My
Yosephine, come board de ship. Long time
Ay vait for you."

ANNA [*Turning on him, sarcastically*] I'm glad
someone's feeling good. [*Wearily*] Gee, I sure wish
we was out of this dump and back in New York.

CHRIS [*With a sigh*] Ay'm glad vhen ve sail
again, too. [*Then, as she makes no comment, he goes
on with a ponderous attempt at sarcasm.*] Ay don't
see vhy you don't like Boston, dough. You have good
time here, Ay tank. You go ashore all time, every day
and night veek ve've been here. You go to movies,

see show, gat all kinds fun—— [*His eyes hard with hatred*] All with that damn Irish fallar!

ANNA [*With weary scorn*] Oh, for heaven's sake, are you off on that again? Where's the harm in his taking me around? D'you want me to sit all day and night in this cabin with you—and knit? Ain't I got a right to have as good a time as I can?

CHRIS It ain't right kind of fun—not with that fallar, no.

ANNA I been back on board every night by eleven, ain't I? [*Then struck by some thought—looks at him with keen suspicion—with rising anger*] Say, look here, what d'you mean by what you yust said?

CHRIS [*Hastily*] Nutting but what Ay say, Anna.

ANNA You said "ain't right" and you said it funny. Say, listen here, you ain't trying to insinuate that there's something wrong between us, are you?

CHRIS [*Horrified*] No. Anna! No, Ay svear to God, Ay never tank dat!

ANNA [*Mollified by his very evident sincerity—sitting down again*] Well, don't you never think it neither if you want me ever to speak to you again. [*Angrily again*] If I ever dreamt you thought that, I'd get the hell out of this barge so quick you couldn't see me for dust.

CHRIS [*Soothingly*] Ay wouldn't never dream —— [*Then after a second's pause, reprovingly*] You vas getting learn to svear. Dat ain't nice for young gel, you tank?

ANNA [*With a faint trace of a smile*] Excuse me. You ain't used to such language, I know. [*Mock-*

## 112  ANNA CHRISTIE

*ingly*] That's what your taking me to sea has done for me.

CHRIS [*Indignantly*] No, it ain't me. It's dat damn sailor fallar learn you bad tangs.

ANNA  He ain't a sailor. He's a stoker.

CHRIS [*Forcibly*] Dat vas million times vorse, Ay tal you! Dem fallars dat vork below shoveling coal vas de dirtiest, rough gang of no-good fallars in vorld!

ANNA  I'd hate to hear you say that to Mat.

CHRIS  Oh, Ay tal him same tang. You don't gat it in head Ay'm scared of him yust 'cause he vas stronger'n Ay vas. [*Menacingly*] You don't gat for fight with fists with dem fallars. Dere's oder vay for fix him.

ANNA [*Glancing at him with sudden alarm*] What d'you mean?

CHRIS [*Sullenly*] Nutting.

ANNA  You'd better not. I wouldn't start no trouble with him if I was you. He might forget some time that you was old and my father—and then you'd be out of luck.

CHRIS [*With smoldering hatred*] Vell, yust let him! Ay'm ole bird maybe, but Ay bet Ay show him trick or two.

ANNA [*Suddenly changing her tone—persuasively*] Aw come on, be good. What's eating you, anyway? Don't you want no one to be nice to me except yourself?

CHRIS [*Placated—coming to her—eagerly*] Yes, Ay do, Anna—only not fallar on sea. But Ay like for you marry steady fallar got good job on land. You have little home in country all your own——

ANNA [*Rising to her feet—brusquely*] Oh, cut it out! [*Scornfully*] Little home in the country! I wish you could have seen the little home in the country where you had me in jail till I was sixteen! [*With rising irritation*] Some day you're going to get me so mad with that talk, I'm going to turn loose on you and tell you—a lot of things that'll open your eyes.

CHRIS [*Alarmed*] Ay don't vant——

ANNA I know you don't; but you keep on talking just the same.

CHRIS Ay don't talk no more den, Anna.

ANNA Then promise me you'll cut out saying nasty things about Mat Burke every chance you get.

CHRIS [*Evasive and suspicious*] Vhy? You like dat faller—very much, Anna?

ANNA Yes, I certainly do! He's a regular man, no matter what faults he's got. One of his fingers is worth all the hundreds of men I met out there—in-land.

CHRIS [*His face darkening*] Maybe you tank you love him, den?

ANNA [*Defiantly*] What of it if I do?

CHRIS [*Scowling and forcing out the words*] Maybe—you tank you—marry him?

ANNA [*Shaking her head*] No! [CHRIS' *face lights up with relief.* ANNA *continues slowly, a trace of sadness in her voice.*] If I'd met him four years ago—or even two years ago—I'd have jumped at the chance, I tell you that straight. And I would now —only he's such a simple guy—a big kid—and I ain't got the heart to fool him. [*She breaks off suddenly.*] But don't ever say again he ain't good enough for me. It's me ain't good enough for him.

CHRIS [*Snorts scornfully*] Py yiminy, you go crazy, Ay tank!

ANNA [*With a mournful laugh*] Well, I been thinking I was myself the last few days. [*She goes and takes a shawl from a hook near the door and throws it over her shoulders.*] Guess I'll take a walk down to the end of the dock for a minute and see what's doing. I love to watch the ships passing. Mat'll be along before long, I guess. Tell him where I am, will you?

CHRIS [*Despondently*] All right, Ay tal him. [ANNA *goes out the doorway in rear.* CHRIS *follows her out and stands on the deck outside for a moment looking after her. Then he comes back inside and shuts the door. He stands looking out of the window—mutters—"Dirty ole davil you." Then he goes to the table, sets the cloth straight mechanically, picks up the newspaper* ANNA *has let fall to the floor and sits down in the rocking-chair. He stares at the paper for a while, then puts it on table, holds his head in his hands and sighs drearily. The noise of a man's heavy footsteps comes from the deck outside and there is a loud knock on the door.* CHRIS *starts, makes a move as if to get up and go to the door, then thinks better of it and sits still. The knock is repeated—then as no answer comes, the door is flung open and* MAT BURKE *appears.* CHRIS *scowls at the intruder and his hand instinctively goes back to the sheath knife on his hip.* BURKE *is dressed up*

—*wears a cheap blue suit, a striped cotton shirt with a black tie, and black shoes newly shined. His face is beaming with good humor.*]

BURKE [*As he sees* CHRIS—*in a jovial tone of mockery*] Well, God bless who's here! [*He bends down and squeezes his huge form through the narrow doorway.*] And how is the world treating you this afternoon, Anna's father?

CHRIS [*Sullenly*] Pooty goot—if it ain't for some fallars.

BURKE [*With a grin*] Meaning me, do you? [*He laughs.*] Well, if you ain't the funny old crank of a man! [*Then soberly*] Where's herself? [CHRIS *sits dumb, scowling, his eyes averted.* BURKE *is irritated by this silence.*] Where's Anna, I'm after asking you?

CHRIS [*Hesitating—then grouchily*] She go down end of dock.

BURKE I'll be going down to her, then. But first I'm thinking I'll take this chance when we're alone to have a word with you. [*He sits down opposite* CHRIS *at the table and leans over toward him.*] And that word is soon said. I'm marrying your Anna before this day is out, and you might as well make up your mind to it whether you like it or no.

CHRIS [*Glaring at him with hatred and forcing a scornful laugh*] Ho-ho! Dat's easy for say!

BURKE You mean I won't? [*Scornfully*] Is it the like of yourself will stop me, are you thinking?

CHRIS Yes, Ay stop it, if it come to vorst.

BURKE [*With scornful pity*] God help you!

CHRIS But ain't no need for me do dat. Anna——

BURKE [*Smiling confidently*] Is it Anna you think will prevent me?

CHRIS  Yes.

BURKE  And I'm telling you she'll not. She knows I'm loving her, and she loves me the same, and I know it.

CHRIS  Ho-ho! She only have fun. She make big fool of you, dat's all!

BURKE [*Unshaken—pleasantly*] That's a lie in your throat, divil mend you!

CHRIS  No, it ain't lie. She tal me yust before she go out she never marry fallar like you.

BURKE  I'll not believe it. 'Tis a great old liar you are, and a divil to be making a power of trouble if you had your way. But 'tis not trouble I'm looking for, and me sitting down here. [*Earnestly*] Let us be talking it out now as man to man. You're her father, and wouldn't it be a shame for us to be at each other's throats like a pair of dogs, and I married with Anna? So out with the truth, man alive. What is it you're holding against me at all?

CHRIS [*A bit placated, in spite of himself, by* BURKE's *evident sincerity—but puzzled and suspicious*] Vell—Ay don't vant for Anna get married. Listen, you fallar. Ay'm a ole man. Ay don't see Anna for fifteen year. She vas all Ay gat in vorld. And now ven she come on first trip—you tank Ay vant her leave me 'lone again?

BURKE [*Heartily*] Let you not be thinking I have no heart at all for the way you'd be feeling.

CHRIS [*Astonished and encouraged—trying to*

*plead persuasively*] Den you do right tang, eh? You ship avay again, leave Anna alone. [*Cajolingly*] Big fallar like you dat's on sea, he don't need vife. He gat new gel in every port, you know dat.

BURKE [*Angrily for a second*] God stiffen you! [*Then controlling himself—calmly*] I'll not be giving you the lie on that. But divil take you, there's a time comes to every man, on sea or land, that isn't a born fool, when he's sick of the lot of them cows, and wearing his heart out to meet up with a fine dacent girl, and have a home to call his own and be rearing up children in it. 'Tis small use you're asking me to leave Anna. She's the wan woman of the world for me, and I can't live without her now, I'm thinking.

CHRIS You forgat all about her in one veek out of port, Ay bet you!

BURKE You don't know the like I am. Death itself wouldn't make me forget her. So let you not be making talk to me about leaving her. I'll not, and be damned to you! It won't be so bad for you as you'd make out at all. She'll be living here in the States, and her married to me. And you'd be seeing her often so—a sight more often than ever you saw her the fifteen years she was growing up in the West. It's quare you'd be the one to be making great trouble about her leaving you when you never laid eyes on her once in all them years.

CHRIS [*Guiltily*] Ay taught it vas better Anna stay away, grow up inland vhere she don't ever know ole davil, sea.

BURKE [*Scornfully*] Is it blaming the sea for your troubles ye are again, God help you? Well, Anna knows it now. 'Twas in her blood, anyway.

CHRIS And Ay don't vant she ever know no-good fallar on sea——

BURKE She knows one now.

CHRIS [*Banging the table with his fist—furiously*] Dat's just it! Dat's yust what you are—no good sailor fallar! You tank Ay lat her life be made sorry by you like her mo'der's vas by me! No, Ay svear! She don't marry you if Ay gat kill you first!

BURKE [*Looks at him a moment, in astonishment—then laughing uproariously*] Ho-ho! Glory be to God, it's bold talk you have for a stumpy runt of a man!

CHRIS [*Threateningly*] Vell—you see!

BURKE [*With grinning defiance*] I'll see, surely! I'll see myself and Anna married this day, I'm telling you. [*Then with contemptuous exasperation*] It's quare fool's blather you have about the sea done this and the sea done that. You'd ought to be 'shamed to be saying the like, and you an old sailor yourself. I'm after hearing a lot of it from you and a lot more that Anna's told me you do be saying to her, and I'm thinking it's a poor weak thing you are, and not a man at all!

CHRIS [*Darkly*] You see if Ay'm man—maybe quicker'n you tank.

BURKE [*Contemptuously*] Yerra, don't be boasting. I'm thinking 'tis out of your wits you've got with fright of the sea. You'd be wishing Anna married to a farmer, she told me. That'd be a swate match, surely! Would you have a fine girl the like of Anna lying down at nights with a muddy scut stinking of pigs and dung? Or would you have her tied for life to the like of them skinny, shriveled swabs does be working in cities?

CHRIS  Dat's lie, you fool!

BURKE  'Tis not. 'Tis your own mad notions I'm after telling. But you know the truth in your heart, if great fear of the sea has made you a liar and coward itself. [*Pounding the table*] The sea's the only life for a man with guts in him isn't afraid of his own shadow! 'Tis only on the sea he's free, and him roving the face of the world, seeing all things, and not giving a damn for saving up money, or stealing from his friends, or any of the black tricks that a land-lubber'd waste his life on. 'Twas yourself knew it once, and you a bosun for years.

CHRIS [*Sputtering with rage*]  You vas crazy fool, Ay tal you!

BURKE  You've swallowed the anchor. The sea gives you a clout once, knocked you down, and you're not man enough to get up for another, but lie there for the rest of your life howling bloody murder. [*Proudly*] Isn't it myself the sea has nearly drowned, and me battered and bate till I was that close to hell I could hear the flames roaring, and never a groan out of me till the sea gave up and it seeing the great strength and guts of a man was in me?

CHRIS [*Scornfully*]  Yes, you vas hell of fallar, hear you tal it!

BURKE [*Angrily*]  You'll be calling me a liar once

too often, me old bucko! Wasn't the whole story of it and my picture itself in the newspapers of Boston a week back? [*Looking* CHRIS *up and down belittlingly*] Sure I'd like to see you in the best of your youth do the like of what I done in the storm and after. 'Tis a mad lunatic, screeching with fear, you'd be this minute!

CHRIS  Ho-ho! You vas young fool! In ole years when Ay vas on windyammer, Ay vas through hundred storms vorse'n dat! Ships vas ships den—and men dat sail on dem vas real men. And now what you gat on steamers? You gat fallars on deck don't know ship from mudscow. [*With a meaning glance at* BURKE] And below deck you gat fallers yust know how for shovel coal—might yust as vell vork on coal vagon ashore!

BURKE [*Stung—angrily*]  Is it casting insults at the men in the stokehole ye are, ye old ape? God stiffen you! Wan of them is worth any ten stock-fish-swilling Squareheads ever shipped on a windbag!

CHRIS [*His face working with rage, his hand going back to the sheath-knife on his hip*]  Irish svine, you!

CHRIS [*Tauntingly*]  Don't ye like the Irish, ye old baboon? 'Tis that you're needing in your family, I'm telling you—an Irishman and a man of the stokehole—to put guts in it so that you'll not be having grandchildren would be fearful cowards and jackasses the like of yourself!

CHRIS [*Half rising from his chair—in a voice choked with rage*]  You look out!

BURKE [*Watching him intently—a mocking smile on his lips*] And it's that you'll be having, no matter what you'll do to prevent; for Anna and me'll be married this day, and no old fool the like of you will stop us when I've made up my mind.

CHRIS [*With a hoarse cry*] You don't! [*He throws himself at* BURKE, *knife in hand, knocking his chair over backwards.* BURKE *springs to his feet quickly in time to meet the attack. He laughs with the pure love of battle. The old Swede is like a child in his hands.* BURKE *does not strike or mistreat him in any way, but simply twists his right hand behind his back and forces the knife from his fingers. He throws the knife into a far corner of the room—tauntingly.*]

BURKE Old men is getting childish shouldn't play with knives. [*Holding the struggling* CHRIS *at arm's length—with a sudden rush of anger, drawing back his fist*] I've half a mind to hit you a great clout will put sense in your square head. Kape off me now, I'm warning you! [*He gives* CHRIS *a push with the flat of his hand which sends the old Swede staggering back against the cabin wall, where he remains standing, panting heavily, his eyes fixed on* BURKE *with hatred, as if he were only collecting his strength to rush at him again.*]

BURKE [*Warningly*] Now don't be coming at me again, I'm saying, or I'll flatten you on the floor with a blow, if 'tis Anna's father you are itself! I've not patience left for you. [*Then with an amused laugh*] Well, 'tis a bold old man you are just the same, and I'd never think it was in you to come tackling me alone. [*A shadow crosses the cabin windows. Both men start.* ANNA *appears in the doorway.*]

ANNA [*With pleased surprise as she sees* BURKE] Hello, Mat. Are you here already? I was down—— [*She stops, looking from one to the other, sensing immediately that something has happened.*] What's up? [*Then noticing the overturned chair—in alarm*] How'd that chair get knocked over? [*Turning on* BURKE *reproachfully*] You ain't been fighting with him, Mat—after you promised?

BURKE [*His old self again*] I've not laid a hand on him, Anna. [*He goes and picks up the chair, then turning on the still questioning* ANNA—*With a reassuring smile*] Let you not be worried at all. 'Twas only a bit of an argument we was having to pass the time till you'd come.

ANNA It must have been some argument when you got to throwing chairs. [*She turns on* CHRIS.] Why don't you say something? What was it about?

CHRIS [*Relaxing at last—avoiding her eyes—sheepishly*] Ve vas talking about ships and fallars on sea.

ANNA [*With a relieved smile*] Oh—the old stuff, eh?

BURKE [*Suddenly seeming to come to a bold decision—with a defiant grin at* CHRIS] He's not after telling you the whole of it. We was arguing about you mostly.

ANNA [*With a frown*] About me?

BURKE And we'll be finishing it out right here and now in your presence if you're willing. [*He sits down at the left of table.*]

ANNA [*Uncertainly—looking from him to her father*] Sure. Tell me what it's all about.

CHRIS [*Advancing toward the table—protesting to* BURKE] No! You don't do dat, you! You tal him you don't vant for hear him talk, Anna.

ANNA But I do. I want this cleared up.

CHRIS [*Miserably afraid now*] Vell, not now, anyvay. You vas going ashore, yes? You ain't got time——

ANNA [*Firmly*] Yes, right here and now. [*She turns to* BURKE] You tell me, Mat, since he don't want to.

BURKE [*Draws a deep breath—then plunges in boldly*] The whole of it's in a few words only. So's he'd make no mistake, and him hating the sight of me, I told him in his teeth I loved you. [*Passionately*] And that's God's truth, Anna, and well you know it!

CHRIS [*Scornfully—forcing a laugh*] Ho-ho! He tal same tang to gel every port he go!

ANNA [*Shrinking from her father with repulsion—resentfully*] Shut up, can't you? [*Then to* BURKE—*feelingly*] I know it's true, Mat. I don't mind what he says.

BURKE [*Humbly grateful*] God bless you!

ANNA And then what?

BURKE And then—— [*Hesitatingly*] And then I said—— [*He looks at her pleadingly*] I said I was sure—I told him I thought you have a bit of love for me, too. [*Passionately*] Say you do, Anna! Let you not destroy me entirely for the love of God! [*He grasps both her hands in his two.*]

ANNA [*Deeply moved and troubled—forcing a trembling laugh*] So you told him that, Mat? No wonder he was mad. [*Forcing out the words*] Well, maybe it's true, Mat. Maybe I do. I been thinking and thinking—I didn't want to, Mat, I'll own up to that—I tried to cut it out—but—— [*She laughs helplessly.*] I guess I can't help it anyhow. So I guess I do, Mat. [*Then with a sudden joyous defiance*] Sure I do! What's the use of kidding myself different? Sure I love you, Mat!

CHRIS [*With a cry of pain*] Anna! [*He sits crushed.*]

BURKE [*With a great depth of sincerity in his humble gratitude*] God be praised!

ANNA [*Assertively*] And I ain't never loved a man in my life before, you can always believe that—no matter what happens.

BURKE [*Goes over to her and puts his arms around her*] Sure I do be believing ivery word you iver said or iver will say. And 'tis you and me will be having a grand, beautiful life together to the end of our days! [*He tries to kiss her. At first she turns away her head—then, overcome by a fierce impulse of passionate love, she takes his head in both her hands and holds his face close to hers, staring into his eyes. Then she kisses him full on the lips.*]

ANNA [*Pushing him away from her—forcing a broken laugh*] Good-by. [*She walks to the doorway in rear—stands with her back toward them, looking out. Her shoulders quiver once or twice as if she were fighting back her sobs.*]

BURKE [*Too in the seventh heaven of bliss to get

*any correct interpretation of her word—with a laugh*] Good-by, is it? The divil you say! I'll be coming back at you in a second for more of the same! [*To* CHRIS, *who has quickened to instant attention at his daughter's good-by, and has looked back at her with a stirring of foolish hope in his eyes*] Now, me old bucko, what'll you be saying? You heard the words from her own lips. Confess I've bate you. Own up like a man when you're bate fair and square. And here's my hand to you—— [*Holds out his hand*] And let you take it and we'll shake and forget what's over and done, and be friends from this out.

CHRIS [*With implacable hatred*] Ay don't shake hands with you fallar—not vhile Ay live!

BURKE [*Offended*] The back of my hand to you then, if that suits you better. [*Growling*] 'Tis a rotten bad loser you are, divil mend you!

CHRIS Ay don't lose. [*Trying to be scornful and self-convincing*] Anna say she like you little bit but you don't hear her say she marry you, Ay bet. [*At the sound of her name* ANNA *has turned round to them. Her face is composed and calm again, but it is the dead calm of despair.*]

BURKE [*Scornfully*] No, and I wasn't hearing her say the sun is shining either.

CHRIS [*Doggedly*] Dat's all right. She don't say it, yust same.

ANNA [*Quietly—coming forward to them*] No, I didn't say it, Mat.

CHRIS [*Eagerly*] Dere! You hear!

BURKE [*Misunderstanding her—with a grin*]

You're waiting till you do be asked, you mane? Well, I'm asking you now. And we'll be married this day, with the help of God!

ANNA [*Gently*] You heard what I said, Mat—after I kissed you?

BURKE [*Alarmed by something in her manner*] No—I disremember.

ANNA I said good-by. [*Her voice trembling*] That kiss was for good-by, Mat.

BURKE [*Terrified*] What d'you mane?

ANNA I can't marry you, Mat—and we've said good-by. That's all.

CHRIS [*Unable to hold back his exultation*] Ay know it! Ay know dat vas so!

BURKE [*Jumping to his feet—unable to believe his ears*] Anna! Is it making game of me you'd be? 'Tis a quare time to joke with me, and don't be doing it, for the love of God.

ANNA [*Looking him in the eyes—steadily*] D'you think I'd kid you? No, I'm not joking, Mat. I mean what I said.

BURKE Ye don't! Ye can't! 'Tis mad you are, I'm telling you!

ANNA [*Fixedly*] No, I'm not.

BURKE [*Desperately*] But what's come over you so sudden? You was saying you loved me——

ANNA I'll say that as often as you want me to. It's true.

BURKE [*Bewilderedly*] Then why—what, in the divil's name—— Oh, God help me, I can't make head or tail to it at all!

ANNA  Because it's the best way out I can figure, Mat. [*Her voice catching*] I been thinking it over and thinking it over day and night all week. Don't think it ain't hard on me, too, Mat.

BURKE  For the love of God, tell me then, what is it that's preventing you wedding me when the two of us has love? [*Suddenly getting an idea and pointing at* CHRIS—*exasperatedly*.] Is it giving heed to the like of that old fool ye are, and him hating me and filling your ears full of bloody lies against me?

CHRIS [*Getting to his feet—raging triumphantly before* ANNA *has a chance to get in a word*]  Yes, Anna believe me, not you! She know her old fa'der don't lie like you.

ANNA [*Turning on her father angrily*]  You sit down, d'you hear? Where do you come in butting in and making things worse? You're like a devil, you are! [*Harshly*] Good Lord, and I was beginning to like you, beginning to forget all I've got held up against you!

CHRIS [*Crushed feebly*]  You ain't got nutting for hold against me, Anna.

ANNA  Ain't I yust! Well, lemme tell you—— [*She glances at* BURKE *and stops abruptly*.] Say, Mat, I'm s'prised at you. You didn't think anything he'd said——

BURKE [*Glumly*]  Sure, what else would it be?

ANNA  Think I've ever paid any attention to all his crazy bull? Gee, you must take me for a five-year-old kid.

BURKE [*Puzzled and beginning to be irritated at her too*] I don't know how to take you, with your saying this one minute and that the next.

ANNA  Well, he has nothing to do with it.

BURKE  Then what is it has? Tell me, and don't keep me waiting and sweating blood.

ANNA [*Resolutely*] I can't tell you—and I won't. I got a good reason—and that's all you need to know. I can't marry you, that's all there is to it. [*Distractedly*] So, for Gawd's sake, let's talk of something else.

BURKE  I'll not! [*Then fearfully*] Is it married to someone else you are—in the West maybe?

ANNA [*Vehemently*]  I should say not.

BURKE [*Regaining his courage*] To the divil with all other reasons then. They don't matter with me at all. [*He gets to his feet confidently, assuming a masterful tone.*] I'm thinking you're the like of them women can't make up their mind till they're drove to it. Well, then, I'll make up your mind for you bloody quick. [*He takes her by the arms, grinning to soften his serious bullying.*] We've had enough of talk! Let you be going into your room now and be dressing in your best and we'll be going ashore.

CHRIS [*Aroused—angrily*] No, py God, she don't do that! [*Takes hold of her arm.*]

ANNA [*Who has listened to* BURKE *in astonishment. She draws away from him, instinctively repelled by his tone, but not exactly sure if he is serious or not—a trace of resentment in her voice*] Say, where do you get that stuff?

BURKE [*Imperiously*] Never mind, now! Let you go get dressed, I'm saying. [*Then turning to* CHRIS] We'll be seeing who'll win in the end—me or you.

CHRIS [*To* ANNA—*also in an authoritative tone*] You stay right here, Anna, you hear! [ANNA *stands looking from one to the other of them as if she thought they had both gone crazy. Then the expression of her face freezes into the hardened sneer of her experience.*]

BURKE [*Violently*] She'll not! She'll do what I say! You've had your hold on her long enough. It's my turn, now.

ANNA [*With a hard laugh*] Your turn? Say, what am I, anyway?

BURKE 'Tis not what you are, 'tis what you're going to be this day—and that's wedded to me before night comes. Hurry up now with your dressing.

CHRIS [*Commandingly*] You don't do one tang he say, Anna! [ANNA *laughs mockingly.*]

BURKE She will, so!

CHRIS Ay tal you she don't! Ay'm her fa'der.

BURKE She will in spite of you. She's taking my orders from this out, not yours.

ANNA [*Laughing again*] Orders is good!

BURKE [*Turning to her impatiently*] Hurry up now, and shake a leg. We've no time to be wasting. [*Irritated as she doesn't move*] Do you hear what I'm telling you?

CHRIS You stay dere, Anna!

ANNA [*At the end of her patience—blazing out at them passionately*] You can go to hell, both of you! [*There is something in her tone that makes them forget their quarrel and turn to her in a stunned amazement.* ANNA *laughs wildly.*] You're just like all the rest of them—you two! Gawd, you'd think I was a piece of furniture! I'll show you! Sit down now! [*As they hesitate—furiously*] Sit down and let me talk for a minute. You're all wrong, see? Listen to me! I'm going to tell you something—and then I'm going to beat it. [*To* BURKE—*with a harsh laugh*] I'm going to tell you a funny story, so pay attention. [*Pointing to* CHRIS] I've been meaning to turn it loose on him every time he'd get my goat with his bull about keeping me safe inland. I wasn't going to tell you, but you've forced me into it. What's the dif? It's all wrong anyway, and you might as well get cured that way as any other. [*With hard mocking*] Only don't forget what you said a minute ago about it not mattering to you what other reason I got so long as I wasn't married to no one else.

BURKE [*Manfully*] That's my word, and I'll stick to it!

ANNA [*Laughing bitterly*] What a chance! You make me laugh, honest! Want to bet you will? Wait 'n see! [*She stands at the table rear, looking from one to the other of the two men with her hard, mocking smile. Then she begins, fighting to control her emotion and speak calmly.*] First thing is, I want to tell you two guys something. You was going on 's if one of you had got to own me. But nobody owns me, see?—'cepting myself. I'll do what I please and no man, I don't give a hoot who he is, can tell me what to do! I ain't asking either of you for a living. I can make it myself—one way or other. I'm my own boss. So put that in your pipe and smoke it! You and your orders!

BURKE [*Protestingly*] I wasn't meaning it that way at all and well you know it. You've no call to be raising this rumpus with me. [*Pointing to* CHRIS] 'Tis him you've a right——

ANNA I'm coming to him. But you—you did mean it that way, too. You sounded—yust like all the rest. [*Hysterically*] But, damn it, shut up! Let me talk for a change!

BURKE 'Tis quare, rough talk, that—for a dacent girl the like of you!

ANNA [*With a hard laugh*] Decent? Who told you I was? [CHRIS *is sitting with bowed shoulders, his head in his hands. She leans over him in exasperation and shakes him violently by the shoulder.*] Don't go to sleep, Old Man! Listen here, I'm talking to you now!

CHRIS [*Straightening up and looking about as if he were seeking a way to escape—with frightened foreboding in his voice*] Ay don't vant for hear it. You vas going out of head, Ay tank, Anna.

ANNA [*Violently*] Well, living with you is enough to drive anyone off their nut. Your bunk about the farm being so fine! Didn't I write you year after year how rotten it was and what a dirty slave them cousins made of me? What'd you care? Nothing! Not even enough to come out and see me! That crazy bull about wanting to keep me away from the sea don't go down with me! You yust didn't want to be bothered with me! You're like all the rest of 'em!

Chris [*Feebly*] Anna! It ain't so——

Anna [*Not heeding his interruption—revengefully*] But one thing I never wrote you. It was one of them cousins that you think is such nice people —the youngest son—Paul—that started me wrong. [*Loudly*] It wasn't none of my fault. I hated him worse'n hell and he knew it. But he was big and strong—[*pointing to* Burke]—like you!

Burke [*Half springing to his feet—his fists clenched*] God blarst it! [*He sinks slowly back in his chair again, the knuckles showing white on his clenched hands, his face tense with the effort to suppress his grief and rage.*]

Chris [*In a cry of horrified pain*] Anna!

Anna [*To him—seeming not to have heard their interruptions*] That was why I run away from the farm. That was what made me get a yob as nurse girl in St. Paul. [*With a hard, mocking laugh*] And you think that was a nice yob for a girl, too, don't you? [*Sarcastically*] With all of them nice inland fellers yust looking for a chance to marry me, I s'pose. Marry me? What a chance! They wasn't looking for marrying. [*As* Burke *lets a groan of fury escape him—desperately*] I'm owning up to everything fair and square. I was caged in, I tell you—yust like in yail— taking care of other people's kids—listening to 'em bawling and crying day and night—when I wanted to be out—and I was lonesome—lonesome as hell! [*With a sudden weariness in her voice*] So I give up finally. What was the use? [*She stops and looks at the two men. Both are motionless and silent.* CHRIS *seems in a stupor of despair, his house of cards fallen about him.* BURKE'S *face is livid with the rage that is eating him up, but he is too stunned and bewildered yet to find a vent for it. The condemnation she feels in their silence goads* ANNA *into a harsh, strident defiance.*] You don't say nothing—either of you—but I know what you're thinking. You're like all the rest! [*To* CHRIS—*furiously*] And who's to blame for it, me or you? If you'd even acted like a man—if you'd even had been a regular father and had me with you—maybe things would be different!

CHRIS [*In agony*]  Don't talk dat vay, Anna! Ay go crazy! Ay von't listen! [*Puts his hands over his ears.*]

ANNA [*Infuriated by his action—stridently*]  You will too listen! [*She leans over and pulls his hands from his ears—with hysterical rage.*] You—keeping me safe inland—I wasn't no nurse girl the last two years—I lied when I wrote you—I was in a house, that's what!—yes, that kind of a house—the kind sailors like you and Mat goes to in port—and your nice inland men, too—and all men, God damn 'em! I hate 'em! Hate 'em! [*She breaks into hysterical sobbing, throwing herself into the chair and hiding her face in her hands on the table. The two men have sprung to their feet.*]

CHRIS [*Whimpering like a child*]  Anna! Anna! It's a lie! It's a lie! [*He stands wringing his hands together and begins to weep.*]

BURKE [*His whole great body tense like a spring—dully and gropingly*] So that's what's in it!

ANNA [*Raising her head at the sound of his voice—with extreme mocking bitterness*] I s'pose you remember your promise, Mat? No other reason was to count with you so long as I wasn't married already. So I s'pose you want me to get dressed and go ashore, don't you? [*She laughs.*] Yes, you do!

BURKE [*On the verge of his outbreak—stammeringly*] God stiffen you!

ANNA [*Trying to keep up her hard, bitter tone, but gradually letting a note of pitiful pleading creep in*] I s'pose I tried to tell you I wasn't—that—no more you'd believe me, wouldn't you? Yes, you would! And if I told you that yust getting out in this barge, and being on the sea had changed me and made me feel different about things, 's if all I'd been through wasn't me and didn't count and was yust like it never happened—you'd laugh, wouldn't you? And you'd die laughing sure if I said that meeting you that funny way that night in the fog, and afterwards seeing that you was straight goods stuck on me, had got me to thinking for the first time, and I sized you up as a different kind of man—a sea man as different from the ones on land as water is from mud—and that was why I got stuck on you, too. I wanted to marry you and fool you, but I couldn't. Don't you see how I've changed? I couldn't marry you with you believing a lie—and I was shamed to tell you the truth—till the both of you forced my hand, and I seen you was the same as all the rest. And now, give me a bawling out and beat it, like I can tell you're going to. [*She stops, looking at* BURKE. *He is silent, his face averted, his features beginning to work with fury. She pleads passionately.*] Will you believe it if I tell you that loving you has made me—clean? It's the straight goods, honest! [*Then as he doesn't reply—bitterly*] Like hell you will! You're like all the rest!

BURKE [*Blazing out—turning on her in a perfect frenzy of rage—his voice trembling with passion*] The rest, is it? God's curse on you! Clane, is it? You slut, you. I'll be killing you now! [*He picks up the chair on which he has been sitting and, swinging it high over his shoulder, springs toward her.* CHRIS *rushes forward with a cry of alarm, trying to ward off the blow from his daughter.* ANNA *looks up into* BURKE'S *eyes with the fearlessness of despair.* BURKE *checks himself, the chair held in the air.*]

CHRIS [*Wildly*] Stop, you crazy fool! You vant for murder her!

ANNA [*Pushing her father away brusquely, her eyes still holding* BURKE'S] Keep out of this, you! [*To* BURKE—*dully*] Well, ain't you got the nerve to do it? Go ahead! I'll be thankful to you, honest. I'm sick of the whole game.

BURKE [*Throwing the chair away into a corner of the room—helplessly*] I can't do it, God help me, and your two eyes looking at me. [*Furiously*] Though I do be thinking I'd have a good right to smash your skull like a rotten egg. Was there iver a woman in the world had the rottenness in her that you have, and was there iver a man the like of me was made the fool of the world, and me thinking thoughts about you, and having great love for you, and dreaming dreams of the fine life we'd have when we'd be wedded! [*His voice high pitched in a lamentation that is like a keen.*] Yerra, God help me! I'm destroyed entirely and my heart is broken in bits! I'm asking God Himself, was it for this He'd have me roaming the earth since I was a lad only, to come to black shame in the end, where I'd be giving a power of love to a woman is the same as others you'd meet in any hooker-shanty in port, with red gowns on them and paint on their grinning mugs, would be sleeping with any man for a dollar or two!

ANNA [*In a scream*] Don't, Mat! For Gawd's sake! [*Then raging and pounding on the table with her hands*] Get out of here! Leave me alone! Get out of here!

BURKE [*His anger rushing back on him*] I'll be going, surely! And I'll be drinking sloos of whisky will wash that black kiss of yours off my lips; and I'll be getting dead rotten drunk so I'll not remember if 'twas iver born you was at all; and I'll be shipping away on some boat will take me to the other end of the world where I'll never see your face again! [*He turns toward the door.*]

CHRIS [*Who has been standing in a stupor—suddenly grasping* BURKE *by the arm—stupidly*] No, you don't go. Ay tank maybe it's better Anna marry you now.

BURKE [*Shaking* CHRIS *off—furiously*] Lave go of me, ye old ape! Marry her, is it? I'd see her roasting in hell first! I'm shipping away out of this, I'm telling you! [*Pointing to* ANNA—*passionately*] And my curse on you and the curse of Almighty God and all the Saints! You've destroyed me this day and may you lie awake in the long nights, tormented with thoughts of Mat Burke and the great wrong you've done him!

ANNA [*In anguish*] Mat! [*But he turns without another word and strides out of the doorway.* ANNA *looks after him wildly, starts to run after him, then hides her face in her outstretched arms, sobbing.* CHRIS *stands in a stupor, staring at the floor.*]

CHRIS [*After a pause, dully*] Ay tank Ay go ashore, too.

ANNA [*Looking up, wildly*] Not after him! Let him go! Don't you dare——

CHRIS [*Somberly*] Ay go for gat drink.

ANNA [*With a harsh laugh*] So I'm driving you to drink, too, eh? I s'pose you want to get drunk so's you can forget—like him?

CHRIS [*Bursting out angrily*] Yes, Ay vant! You tank Ay like hear dem tangs. [*Breaking down—weeping*] Ay tank you vasn't dat kind of gel, Anna.

ANNA [*Mockingly*] And I s'pose you want me to beat it, don't you? You don't want me here disgracing you, I s'pose?

CHRIS No, you stay here! [*Goes over and pats her on the shoulder, the tears running down his face.*] Ain't your fault, Anna, Ay know dat. [*She looks up at him, softened. He bursts into rage.*] It's dat ole davil, sea, do this to me! [*He shakes his fist at the door.*] It's her dirty tricks! It vas all right on barge with yust you and me. Den she bring dat Irish fallar in fog, she make you like him, she make you fight with me all time! If dat Irish fallar don't never come, you don't never tal me dem tangs, Ay don't never know, and everytang's all right. [*He shakes his fist again.*] Dirty ole davil!

ANNA [*With spent weariness*] Oh, what's the use? Go on ashore and get drunk.

CHRIS [*Goes into room on left and gets his cap. He goes to the door, silent and stupid—then turns*] You vait here, Anna?

ANNA [*Dully*] Maybe—and maybe not. Maybe I'll get drunk too. Maybe I'll—— But what the hell do you care what I do? Go on and beat it. [CHRIS *turns stupidly and goes out.* ANNA *sits at the table, staring straight in front of her.*]

[*The curtain falls.*]

# ACT FOUR

SCENE *Same as Act Three, about nine o'clock of a foggy night two days later. The whistles of steamers in the harbor can be heard. The cabin is lighted by a small lamp on the table. A suit case stands in the middle of the floor.* ANNA *is sitting in the rocking-chair. She wears a hat, is all dressed up as in Act One. Her face is pale, looks terribly tired and worn, as if the two days just past had been ones of suffering and sleepless nights. She stares before her despondently, her chin in her hands. There is a timid knock on the door in rear.* ANNA *jumps to her feet with a startled exclamation and looks toward the door with an expression of mingled hope and fear.*

ANNA [*Faintly*] Come in. [*Then summoning her courage—more resolutely*] Come in. [*The door is opened and* CHRIS *appears in the doorway. He is in a very bleary, bedraggled condition, suffering from the after-effects of his drunk. A tin pail full of foam-*

*ing beer is in his hand. He comes forward, his eyes avoiding* ANNA'S. *He mutters stupidly.*] It's foggy.

ANNA [*Looking him over with contempt*] So you come back at last, did you? You're a fine looking sight! [*Then jeeringly*] I thought you'd beaten it for good on account of the disgrace I'd brought on you.

CHRIS [*Wincing—faintly*] Don't say dat, Anna, please! [*He sits in a chair by the table, setting down the can of beer, holding his head in his hands.*]

ANNA [*Looks at him with a certain sympathy*] What's the trouble? Feeling sick?

CHRIS [*Dully*] Inside my head feel sick.

ANNA Well, what d'you expect after being soused for two days? [*Resentfully*] It serves you right. A fine thing—you leaving me alone on this barge all that time!

CHRIS [*Humbly*] Ay'm sorry, Anna.

ANNA [*Scornfully*] Sorry!

CHRIS But Ay'm not sick inside head vay you mean. Ay'm sick from tank too much about you, about me.

ANNA And how about me? D'you suppose I ain't been thinking, too?

CHRIS Ay'm sorry, Anna. [*He sees her bag and gives a start.*] You pack your bag, Anna? You vas going——?

ANNA [*Forcibly*] Yes, I was going right back to what you think.

CHRIS Anna!

ANNA I went ashore to get a train for New York. I'd been waiting and waiting till I was sick of it. Then I changed my mind and decided not to go today. But I'm going first thing tomorrow, so it'll all be the same in the end.

CHRIS [*Raising his head—pleadingly*] No, you never do dat, Anna!

ANNA [*With a sneer*] Why not, I'd like to know?

CHRIS You don't never gat to do—dat vay—no more, Ay tal you. Ay fix dat up all right.

ANNA [*Suspiciously*] Fix what up?

CHRIS [*Not seeming to have heard her question—sadly*] You vas vaiting, you say? You vasn't vaiting for me, Ay bet.

ANNA [*Callously*] You'd win.

CHRIS For dat Irish fallar?

ANNA [*Defiantly*] Yes—if you want to know! [*Then with a forlorn laugh*] If he did come back it'd only be 'cause he wanted to beat me up or kill me, I suppose. But even if he did, I'd rather have him come than not show up at all. I wouldn't care what he did.

CHRIS Ay guess it's true you vas in love with him all right.

ANNA You guess!

CHRIS [*Turning to her earnestly*] And Ay'm sorry for you like hell he don't come, Anna!

ANNA [*Softened*] Seems to me you've changed your tune a lot.

CHRIS Ay've been tanking, and Ay guess it vas all my fault—all bad tangs dat happen to you. [*Pleadingly*] You try for not hate me, Anna. Ay'm crazy ole fool, dat's all.

ANNA Who said I hated you?

CHRIS Ay'm sorry for everytang Ay do wrong for

you, Anna. Ay vant for you to be happy all rest of your life for make up! It make you happy marry dat Irish fallar, Ay vant it, too.

ANNA [*Dully*] Well, there ain't no chance. But I'm glad you think different about it, anyway.

CHRIS [*Supplicatingly*] And you tank—maybe —you forgive me sometime?

ANNA [*With a wan smile*] I'll forgive you right now.

CHRIS [*Seizing her hand and kissing it—brokenly*] Anna lilla! Anna lilla!

ANNA [*Touched but a bit embarrassed*] Don't bawl about it. There ain't nothing to forgive, anyway. It ain't your fault, and it ain't mine, and it ain't his neither. We're all poor nuts, and things happen, and we yust get mixed in wrong, that's all.

CHRIS [*Eagerly*] You say right tang, Anna, py golly! It ain't nobody's fault! [*Shaking his fist*] It's dat ole davil sea!

ANNA [*With an exasperated laugh*] Gee, won't you ever can that stuff? [CHRIS *relapses into injured silence. After a pause* ANNA *continues curiously*] You said a minute ago you'd fixed something up— about me. What was it?

CHRIS [*After a hesitating pause*] Ay'm shipping avay on sea again, Anna.

ANNA [*Astounded*] You're—what?

CHRIS Ay sign on steamer sail tomorrow. Ay gat my ole yob—bosun. [ANNA *stares at him. As he goes on, a bitter smiles comes over her face.*] Ay tank dat's best tang for you. Ay only bring you bad luck, Ay tank. Ay make your mo'der's life sorry. Ay don't vant make yours dat vay, but Ay do yust same. Dat ole davil, sea, she make me Yonah man ain't no good for nobody. And Ay tank now it ain't no use fight with sea. No man dat live going to beat her, py yingo!

ANNA [*With a laugh of helpless bitterness*] So that's how you've fixed me, is it?

CHRIS Yes, Ay tank if dat ole davil gat me back she leave you alone den.

ANNA [*Bitterly*] But, for Gawd's sake, don't you see you're doing the same thing you've always done? Don't you see——? [*But she sees the look of obsessed stubbornness on her father's face and gives it up helplessly.*] But what's the use of talking? You ain't right, that's what. I'll never blame you for nothing no more. But how you could figure out that was fixing me——!

CHRIS Dat ain't all. Ay gat dem fallars in steamship office to pay you all money coming to me every month vhile Ay'm avay.

ANNA [*With a hard laugh*] Thanks. But I guess I won't be hard up for no small change.

CHRIS [*Hurt—humbly*] It ain't much, Ay know, but it's plenty for keep you so you never gat go back——

ANNA [*Shortly*] Shut up, will you? We'll talk about it later, see?

CHRIS [*After a pause—ingratiatingly*] You like Ay go ashore look for dat Irish fallar, Anna?

ANNA [*Angrily*] Not much! Think I want to drag him back?

CHRIS [*After a pause—uncomfortably*] Py golly,

dat booze don't go vell. Give me fever, Ay tank. Ay feel hot like hell. [*He takes off his coat and lets it drop on the floor. There is a loud thud.*]

ANNA [*With a start*] What you got in your pocket, for Pete's sake—a ton of lead? [*She reaches down, takes the coat and pulls out a revolver—looks from it to him in amazement.*] A gun? What were you doing with this?

CHRIS [*Sheepishly*] Ah forget. Ain't nothing. Ain't loaded, anyvay.

ANNA [*Breaking it open to make sure—then closing it again—looking at him suspiciously*] That ain't telling me why you got it?

CHRIS Ay'm ole fool. Ay got it when Ay go ashore first. Ay tank den it's all fault of dat Irish fallar.

ANNA [*With a shudder*] Say, you're crazier than I thought. I never dreamt you'd go that far.

CHRIS [*Quickly*] Ah don't. Ay gat better sense right avay. Ay don't never buy bullets even. It ain't his fault, Ay know.

ANNA [*Still suspicious of him*] Well, I'll take care of this for a while, loaded or not. [*She puts it in the drawer of table and closes the drawer.*]

CHRIS [*Placatingly*] Throw it overboard if you vant. Ay don't care. [*Then after a pause*] Py golly, Ay tank Ay go lie down. Ay feel sick. [ANNA *takes a magazine from the table.* CHRIS *hesitates by her chair.*] Ve talk again before Ay go, yes?

ANNA [*Dully*] Where's this ship going to?

CHRIS Cape Town. Dat's in South Africa. She's British steamer called Londonderry. [*He stands hesi-*

*tatingly—finally blurts out*] Anna—you forgive me sure?

ANNA [*Wearily*] Sure I do. You ain't to blame. You're yust—what you are—like me.

CHRIS [*Pleadingly*] Den—you lat me kiss you again once?

ANNA [*Raising her face—forcing a wan smile*] Sure. No hard feelings.

CHRIS [*Kisses her brokenly*] Anna lilla! Ay—— [*He fights for words to express himself, but finds none—miserably—with a sob*] Ay can't say it. Goodnight, Anna.

ANNA Good-night. [*He picks up the can of beer and goes slowly into the room on left, his shoulders bowed, his head sunk forward dejectedly. He closes the door after him.* ANNA *turns over the pages of the magazine, trying desperately to banish her thoughts by looking at the pictures. This fails to distract her, and flinging the magazine back on the table, she springs to her feet and walks about the cabin distractedly, clenching and unclenching her hands. She speaks aloud to herself in a tense, trembling voice.*] Gawd, I can't stand this much longer! What am I waiting for anyway?—like a damn fool! [*She laughs helplessly, then checks herself abruptly, as she hears the sound of heavy footsteps on the deck outside. She appears to recognize these and her face lights up with joy. She gasps.*] Mat! [*A strange terror seems suddenly to seize her. She rushes to the table, takes the revolver out of drawer and crouches down in the corner, left, behind the cupboard. A moment later the door is flung open and* MAT BURKE *appears in the doorway. He is in bad shape—his clothes torn and dirty, covered with sawdust as if he had been grovelling or sleeping on barroom floors. There is a red bruise on his forehead over one of his eyes, another over one cheekbone, his knuckles are skinned and raw—plain evidence of the fighting he has been through on his "bat." His eyes are bloodshot and heavy-lidded, his face has a bloated look. But beyond these appearances—the results of heavy drinking—there is an expression in his eyes of wild mental turmoil, of impotent animal rage baffled by its own abject misery.*]

BURKE [*Peers blinkingly about the cabin—hoarsely*] Let you not be hiding from me, whoever's here—though 'tis well you know I'd have a right to come back and murder you. [*He stops to listen. Hearing no sound, he closes the door behind him and comes forward to the table. He throws himself into the rocking-chair—despondently.*] There's no one here, I'm thinking, and 'tis a great fool I am to be coming. [*With a sort of dumb, uncomprehending anguish*] Yerra, Mat Burke, 'tis a great jackass you've become and what's got into you at all, at all? She's gone out of this long ago, I'm telling you, and you'll never see her face again. [ANNA *stands up, hesitating, struggling between joy and fear.* BURKE's *eyes fall on* ANNA's *bag. He leans over to examine it.*] What's this? [*Joyfully*] It's hers. She's not gone! But where is she? Ashore? [*Darkly*] What would she be doing ashore on this rotten night? [*His face suddenly convulsed with grief and rage.*] 'Tis that, is it? Oh, God's curse on her. [*Raging*] I'll wait till she comes and choke her dirty life out. [ANNA *starts, her face grows hard. She steps into the room, the revolver in her right hand by her side.*]

ANNA [*In a cold, hard tone*] What are you doing here?

BURKE [*Wheeling about with a terrified gasp*] Glory be to God! [*They remain motionless and silent for a moment, holding each other's eyes.*]

ANNA [*In the same hard voice*] Well, can't you talk?

BURKE [*Trying to fall into an easy, careless tone*] You've a year's growth scared out of me, coming at me so sudden and me thinking I was alone.

ANNA You've got your nerve butting in here without knocking or nothing. What d'you want?

BURKE [*Airily*] Oh, nothing much. I was wanting to have a last word with you, that's all. [*He moves a step toward her.*]

ANNA [*Sharply—raising the revolver in her hand*] Careful now! Don't try getting too close. I heard what you said you'd do to me.

BURKE [*Noticing the revolver for the first time*] Is it murdering me you'd be now, God forgive you? [*Then with a contemptuous laugh*] Or is it thinking I'd be frightened by that old tin whistle? [*He walks straight for her.*]

ANNA [*Wildly*] Look out, I tell you!

BURKE [*Who has come so close that the revolver is almost touching his chest*] Let you shoot, then! [*Then with sudden wild grief*] Let you shoot, I'm saying, and be done with it! Let you end me with a shot and I'll be thanking you, for it's a rotten dog's life I've lived the past two days since I've known what you are, till I'm after wishing I was never born at all!

ANNA [*Overcome—letting the revolver drop to the floor, as if her fingers had no strength to hold it—hysterically*] What d'you want coming here? Why don't you beat it? Go on! [*She passes him and sinks down in the rocking-chair.*]

BURKE [*Following her—mournfully*] 'Tis right you'd be asking why did I come. [*Then angrily*] 'Tis because 'tis a great weak fool of the world I am, and me tormented with the wickedness you'd told of yourself, and drinking oceans of booze that'd make me forget. Forget? Divil a word I'd forget, and your face grinning always in front of my eyes, awake or asleep, till I do be thinking a madhouse is the proper place for me.

ANNA [*Glancing at his hands and face—scornfully*] You look like you ought to be put away some place. Wonder you wasn't pulled in. You been scrapping, too, ain't you?

BURKE I have—with every scut would take off his coat to me! [*Fiercely*] And each time I'd be hitting one a clout in the mug, it wasn't his face I'd be seeing at all, but yours, and me wanting to drive you a blow would knock you out of this world where I wouldn't be seeing or thinking more of you.

ANNA [*Her lips trembling pitifully*] Thanks!

BURKE [*Walking up and down—distractedly*] That's right, make game of me! Oh, I'm a great coward surely, to be coming back to speak with you at all. You've a right to laugh at me.

ANNA  I ain't laughing at you, Mat.

BURKE [*Unheeding*]  You to be what you are, and me to be Mat Burke, and me to be drove back to look at you again! 'Tis black shame is on me!

ANNA [*Resentfully*]  Then get out. No one's holding you!

BURKE [*Bewilderedly*]  And me to listen to that talk from a woman like you and be frightened to close her mouth with a slap! Oh, God help me, I'm a yellow coward for all men to spit at! [*Then furiously*] But I'll not be getting out of this till I've had me word. [*Raising his fist threateningly*] And let you look out how you drive me! [*Letting his fist fall helplessly*] Don't be angry now! I'm raving like a real lunatic, I'm thinking, and the sorrow you put on me has my brains drownded in grief. [*Suddenly bending down to her and grasping her arm intensely*] Tell me it's a lie, I'm saying! That's what I'm after coming to hear you say.

ANNA [*Dully*]  A lie? What?

BURKE [*With passionate entreaty*]  All the badness you told me two days back. Sure it must be a lie! You was only making game of me, wasn't you? Tell me 'twas a lie, Anna, and I'll be saying prayers of thanks on my two knees to the Almighty God!

ANNA [*Terribly shaken—faintly*]  I can't, Mat. [*As he turns away—imploringly*] Oh, Mat, won't you see that no matter what I was I ain't that any more? Why, listen! I packed up my bag this afternoon and went ashore. I'd been waiting here all alone for two days, thinking maybe you'd come back —thinking maybe you'd think over all I'd said—and maybe—oh, I don't know what I was hoping! But I was afraid to even go out of the cabin for a second, honest—afraid you might come and not find me here. Then I gave up hope when you didn't show up and I went to the railroad station. I was going to New York. I was going back——

BURKE [*Hoarsely*] God's curse on you!

ANNA Listen, Mat. You hadn't come, and I'd gave up hope. But—in the station—I couldn't go. I'd bought my ticket and everything. [*She takes the ticket from her dress and tries to hold it before his eyes.*] But I got to thinking about you—and I couldn't take the train—I couldn't! So I come back here—to wait some more. Oh, Mat, don't you see I've changed? Can't you forgive what's dead and gone—and forget it?

BURKE [*Turning on her—overcome by rage again*] Forget, is it? I'll not forget till my dying day, I'm telling you, and me tormented with thoughts. [*In a frenzy*] Oh, I'm wishing I had wan of them fornenst me this minute and I'd beat him with my fists till he'd be a bloody corpse! I'm wishing the whole lot of them will roast in hell till the Judgment Day—and yourself along with them, for you're as bad as they are.

ANNA [*Shuddering*] Mat! [*Then after a pause—in a voice of dead, stony calm*] Well, you've had your say. Now you better beat it.

BURKE [*Starts slowly for the door—hesitates—then after a pause*] And what'll you be doing?

ANNA What difference does it make to you?

BURKE   I'm asking you!

ANNA [*In the same tone*]   My bag's packed and I got my ticket. I'll go to New York tomorrow.

BURKE [*Helplessly*]   You mean—you'll be doing the same again?

ANNA [*Stonily*]   Yes.

BURKE [*In anguish*]   You'll not! Don't torment me with that talk! 'Tis a she-divil you are sent to drive me mad entirely!

ANNA [*Her voice breaking*]   Oh, for Gawd's sake, Mat, leave me alone! Go away! Don't you see I'm licked? Why d'you want to keep on kicking me?

BURKE [*Indignantly*]   And don't you deserve the worst I'd say, God forgive you?

ANNA   All right. Maybe I do. But don't rub it in. Why ain't you done what you said you was going to? Why ain't you got that ship was going to take you to the other side of the earth where you'd never see me again?

BURKE   I have.

ANNA [*Startled*]   What—then you're going—honest?

BURKE   I signed on today at noon, drunk as I was—and she's sailing tomorrow.

ANNA   And where's she going to?

BURKE   Cape Town.

ANNA [*The memory of having heard that name a little while before coming to her—with a start, confusedly*]   Cape Town? Where's that? Far away?

BURKE   'Tis at the end of Africa. That's far for you.

ANNA [*Forcing a laugh*] You're keeping your word all right, ain't you? [*After a slight pause—curiously*] What's the boat's name?

BURKE  The Londonderry.

ANNA [*It suddenly comes to her that this is the same ship her father is sailing on.*] The Londonderry! It's the same—Oh, this is too much! [*With wild, ironical laughter*]. Ha-ha-ha!

BURKE  What's up with you now?

ANNA  Ha-ha-ha! It's funny, funny! I'll die laughing!

BURKE [*Irritated*] Laughing at what?

ANNA  It's a secret. You'll know soon enough. It's funny. [*Controlling herself—after a pause—cynically*] What kind of a place is this Cape Town? Plenty of dames there, I suppose?

BURKE  To hell with them! That I may never see another woman to my dying hour!

ANNA  That's what you say now, but I'll bet by the time you get there you'll have forgot all about me and start in talking the same old bull you talked to me to the first one you meet.

BURKE [*Offended*] I'll not, then! God mend you, is it making me out to be the like of yourself you are, and you taking up with this one and that all the years of your life?

ANNA [*Angrily assertive*] Yes, that's yust what I do mean! You been doing the same thing all your life, picking up a new girl in every port. How're you any better than I was?

BURKE [*Thoroughly exasperated*] Is it no shame you have at all? I'm a fool to be wasting talk on you and you hardened in badness. I'll go out of this and leave you alone forever. [*He starts for the door—then stops to turn on her furiously.*] And I suppose 'tis the same lies you told them all before that you told to me?

ANNA [*Indignantly*] That's a lie! I never did!

BURKE [*Miserably*] You'd be saying that, anyway.

ANNA [*Forcibly, with growing intensity*] Are you trying to accuse me—of being in love—really in love—with them?

BURKE I'm thinking you were, surely.

ANNA [*Furiously, as if this were the last insult—advancing on him threateningly*] You mutt, you! I've stood enough from you. Don't you dare. [*With scornful bitterness*] Love 'em! Oh, my Gawd! You damn thick-head! Love 'em? [*Savagely*] I hated 'em, I tell you! Hated 'em, hated 'em, hated 'em! And may Gawd strike me dead this minute and my mother, too, if she was alive, if I ain't telling you the honest truth!

BURKE [*Immensely pleased by her vehemence—a light beginning to break over his face—but still uncertain, torn between doubt and the desire to believe—helplessly*] If I could only be believing you now!

ANNA [*Distractedly*] Oh, what's the use? What's the use of me talking? What's the use of anything? [*Pleadingly*] Oh, Mat, you mustn't think that for a second! You mustn't! Think all the other bad about me you want to, and I won't kick, 'cause you've a right to. But don't think that! [*On the point of tears*] I couldn't bear it! It's be yust too much to know you was going away where I'd never see you again—thinking that about me!

BURKE [*After an inward struggle—tensely—forcing out the words with difficulty*] If I was believing—that you'd never had love for any other man in the world but me—I could be forgetting the rest, maybe.

ANNA [*With a cry of joy*] Mat!

BURKE [*Slowly*] If 'tis truth you're after telling, I'd have a right, maybe, to believe you'd changed—and that I'd changed you myself till the thing you'd been all your life wouldn't be you any more at all.

ANNA [*Hanging on his words—breathlessly*] Oh, Mat! That's what I been trying to tell you all along!

BURKE [*Simply*] For I've a power of strength in me to lead men the way I want, and women, too, maybe, and I'm thinking I'd change you to a new woman entirely, so I'd never know, or you either, what kind of woman you'd been in the past at all.

ANNA Yes, you could, Mat! I know you could!

BURKE And I'm thinking 'twasn't your fault, maybe, but having that old ape for a father that left you to grow up alone, made you what you was. And if I could be believing 'tis only me you——

ANNA [*Distractedly*] You got to believe it, Mat! What can I do? I'll do anything, anything you want to prove I'm not lying!

BURKE [*Suddenly seems to have a solution. He feels in the pocket of his coat and grasps something —solemnly*] Would you be willing to swear an oath, now—a terrible, fearful oath would send your soul to the divils in hell if you was lying?

ANNA [*Eagerly*] Sure, I'll swear, Mat—on anything!

BURKE [*Takes a small, cheap old crucifix from his pocket and holds it up for her to see*] Will you swear on this?

ANNA [*Reaching out for it*] Yes. Sure I will. Give it to me.

BURKE [*Holding it away*] 'Tis a cross was given me by my mother, God rest her soul. [*He makes the sign of the cross mechanically.*] I was a lad only, and she told me to keep it by me if I'd be waking or sleeping and never lose it, and it'd bring me luck. She died soon after. But I'm after keeping it with me from that day to this, and—I'm telling you there's great power in it, and 'tis great bad luck it's saved me from and me roaming the seas, and I have it tied round my neck when my last ship sunk, and it bringing me safe to land when the others went to their death. [*Very earnestly*] And I'm warning you now, if you'd swear an oath on this, 'tis my old woman herself will be looking down from Hivin above, and praying Almighty God and the Saints to put a great curse on you if she'd hear you swearing a lie!

ANNA [*Awed by his manner—superstitiously*] I wouldn't have the nerve—honest—if it was a lie. But it's the truth and I ain't scared to swear. Give it to me.

BURKE [*Handing it to her—almost frightenedly, as if he feared for her safety*] Be careful what you'd swear. I'm saying.

ANNA [*Holding the cross gingerly*] Well—what do you want me to swear? You say it.

BURKE  Swear I'm the only man in the world ivir you felt love for.

ANNA [*Looking into his eyes steadily*]  I swear it.

BURKE  And that you'll be forgetting from this day all the badness you've done and never do the like of it again.

ANNA [*Forcibly*]  I swear it! I swear it by God!

BURKE  And may the blackest curse of God strike you if you're lying. Say it now!

ANNA  And may the blackest curse of God strike me if I'm lying!

BURKE [*With a stupendous sigh*]  Oh, glory be to God, I'm after believing you now! [*He takes the cross from her hand, his face beaming with joy, and puts it back in his pocket. He puts his arm about her waist and is about to kiss her when he stops, appalled by some terrible doubt.*]

ANNA [*Alarmed*]  What's the matter with you?

BURKE [*With sudden fierce questioning*]  Is it Catholic ye are?

ANNA [*Confused*]  No. Why?

BURKE [*Filled with a sort of bewildered foreboding*]  Oh, God, help me! [*With a dark glance of suspicion at her.*] There's some divil's trickery in it, to be swearing an oath on a Catholic cross and you wan of the others.

ANNA [*Distractedly*]  Oh, Mat, don't you believe me?

BURKE [*Miserably*]  If it isn't a Catholic you are——

ANNA  I ain't nothing. What's the difference? Didn't you hear me swear?

BURKE [*Passionately*] Oh, I'd a right to stay away from you—but I couldn't! I was loving you in spite of it all and wanting to be with you, God forgive me, no matter what you are. I'd go mad if I'd not have you! I'd be killing the world—— [*He seizes her in his arms and kisses her fiercely.*]

ANNA [*With a gasp of joy*] Mat!

BURKE [*Suddenly holding her away from him and staring into her eyes as if to probe into her soul—slowly*] If your oath is no proper oath at all, I'll have to be taking your naked word for it and have you anyway, I'm thinking—I'm needing you that bad!

ANNA [*Hurt—reproachfully*] Mat! I swore, didn't I?

BURKE [*Defiantly, as if challenging fate*] Oath or no oath, 'tis no matter. We'll be wedded in the morning, with the help of God. [*Still more defiantly*]. We'll be happy now, the two of us, in spite of the divil! [*He crushes her to him and kisses her again. The door on the left is pushed open and* CHRIS *appears in the doorway. He stands blinking at them. At first the old expression of hatred of* BURKE *comes into his eyes instinctively. Then a look of resignation and relief takes its place. His face lights up with a sudden happy thought. He turns back into the bedroom—reappears immediately with the tin can of beer in his hand—grinning.*]

CHRIS Ve have a drink on this, py golly! [*They break away from each other with startled exclamations.*]

## 158  ANNA CHRISTIE

BURKE [*Explosively*] God stiffen it! [*He takes a step toward* CHRIS *threateningly.*]

ANNA [*Happily—to her father*] That's the way to talk! [*With a laugh*] And say, it's about time for you and Mat to kiss and make up. You're going to be shipmates on the *Londonderry,* did you know it?

BURKE [*Astounded*] Shipmates—— Has himself——

CHRIS [*Equally astounded*] Ay vas bosun on her.

BURKE The divil! [*Then angrily*] You'd be going back to sea and leaving her alone, would you?

ANNA [*Quickly*] It's all right, Mat. That's where he belongs, and I want him to go. You got to go, too; we'll need the money. [*With a laugh, as she gets the glasses*] And as for me being alone, that runs in the family, and I'll get used to it. [*Pouring out their glasses*] I'll get a little house somewhere and I'll make a regular place for you two to come back to,— wait and see. And now you drink up and be friends.

BURKE [*Happily—but still a bit resentful against the old man*] Sure! [*Clinking his glass against* CHRIS'.] Here's luck to you! [*He drinks.*]

CHRIS [*Subdued—his face melancholy*] Skoal. [*He drinks.*]

BURKE [*To* ANNA, *with a wink*] You'll not be lonesome long. I'll see to that, with the help of God. 'Tis himself here will be having a grandchild to ride on his foot, I'm telling you!

ANNA [*Turning away in embarrassment*] Quit the kidding now. [*She picks up her bag and goes into the room on left. As soon as she is gone* BURKE *relapses into an attitude of gloomy thought.* CHRIS *stares at his beer absent-mindedly. Finally* BURKE *turns on him.*]

BURKE  Is it any religion at all you have, you and your Anna?

CHRIS [*Surprised*]  Vhy yes. Ve vas Lutheran in ole country.

BURKE [*Horrified*]  Luthers, is it? [*Then with a grim resignation, slowly, aloud to himself*]  Well, I'm damned then surely. Yerra, what's the difference? 'Tis the will of God, anyway.

CHRIS [*Moodily preoccupied with his own thoughts—speaks with somber premonition as* ANNA *re-enters from the left*]  It's funny. It's queer, yes—you and me shipping on same boat dat vay. It ain't right. Ay don't know—it's dat funny vay ole davil sea do her vorst dirty tricks, yes. It's so. [*He gets up and goes back and, opening the door, stares out into the darkness.*]

BURKE [*Nodding his head in gloomy acquiescence—with a great sigh*]  I'm fearing maybe you have the right of it for once, divil take you.

ANNA [*Forcing a laugh*]  Gee, Mat, you ain't agreeing with him, are you? [*She comes forward and puts her arm about his shoulder—with a determined gayety.*]  Aw say, what's the matter? Cut out the gloom. We're all fixed now, ain't we, me and you? [*Pours out more beer into his glass and fills one for herself—slaps him on the back.*]  Come on! Here's to the sea, no matter what! Be a game sport and drink to that! Come on! [*She gulps down her glass.* BURKE *banishes his superstitious premonitions with a defiant jerk of his head, grins up at her, and drinks to her toast.*]

CHRIS [*Looking out into the night—lost in his somber preoccupation—shakes his head and mutters*] Fog, fog, fog, all bloody time. You can't see vhere you vas going, no. Only dat ole davil, sea—she knows! [*The two stare at him. From the harbor comes the muffled, mournful wail of steamers' whistles.*]

[*The curtain falls.*]

# THE HAIRY APE

---

*A Comedy of Ancient and Modern
Life in Eight Scenes*

# CHARACTERS

ROBERT SMITH, "YANK"
PADDY
LONG
MILDRED DOUGLAS
HER AUNT
SECOND ENGINEER
A GUARD
A SECRETARY OF AN ORGANIZATION
STOKERS, LADIES, GENTLEMEN, ETC.

# SCENES

Scene I — The firemen's forecastle of an ocean liner an hour after sailing from New York.

Scene II — Section of promenade deck, two days out—morning.

Scene III — The stokehole. A few minutes later.

Scene IV — Same as Scene I. Half an hour later.

Scene V — Fifth Avenue, New York. Three weeks later.

Scene VI — An island near the city. The next night.

Scene VII — In the city. About a month later.

Scene VIII — In the city. Twilight of the next day.

# THE HAIRY APE

## SCENE ONE

SCENE *The firemen's forecastle of a transatlantic liner an hour after sailing from New York for the voyage across. Tiers of narrow, steel bunks, three deep, on all sides. An entrance in rear. Benches on the floor before the bunks. The room is crowded with men, shouting, cursing, laughing, singing—a confused, inchoate uproar swelling into a sort of unity, a meaning—the bewildered, furious, baffled defiance of a beast in a cage. Nearly all the men are drunk. Many bottles are passed from hand to hand. All are dressed in dungaree pants, heavy ugly shoes. Some wear singlets, but the majority are stripped to the waist.*

*The treatment of this scene, or of any other scene in the play, should by no means be naturalistic. The effect sought after is a cramped space in the bowels of a ship, imprisoned by white steel. The lines of bunks, the uprights supporting them, cross each other like the steel framework of a cage. The ceiling crushes down upon the men's heads. They cannot stand upright. This accentuates the natural stooping posture which shoveling coal and the resultant overdevelopment of back and shoulder muscles have given them. The men themselves should resemble those pictures in which the appearance of Neanderthal Man is guessed at. All are hairy-chested, with long arms of tremendous power, and low, receding brows above their small, fierce, resentful eyes. All the civilized white races are represented, but except for the slight differentiation in color of hair, skin, eyes, all these men are alike.*

*The curtain rises on a tumult of sound.* YANK *is seated in the foreground. He seems broader, fiercer, more truculent, more powerful, more sure of himself than the rest. They respect his superior strength—the grudging respect of fear. Then, too, he represents to them a self-expression, the very last word in what they are, their most highly developed individual.*

VOICES   Gif me trink dere, you!
        'Ave a wet!
        Salute!
        Gesundheit!
        Skoal!
        Drunk as a lord, God stiffen you!
        Here's how!

## THE HAIRY APE 167

Luck!
Pass back that bottle, damn you!
Pourin' it down his neck!
Ho, Froggy! Where the devil have you been?
*La Touraine.*
I hit him smash in yaw, py Gott!
Jenkins—the First—he's a rotten swine——
And the coppers nabbed him—and I run——
I like peer better. It don't pig head gif you.
A slut, I'm sayin'. She robbed me aslape—
To hell with 'em all!
You're a bloody liar!
Say dot again! (*Commotion. Two men about to fight are pulled apart.*]
No scrappin' now!
Tonight——
See who's the best man!
Bloody Dutchman!
Tonight on the for'ard square.
I'll bet on Dutchy.
He packa da wallop, I tell you!
Shut up, Wop!
No fightin', maties. We're all chums, ain't we?
[*A voice starts bawling a song.*]
"Beer, beer, glorious beer!
Fill yourselves right up to here."

YANK [*For the first time seeming to take notice of the uproar about him, turns around threateningly—in a tone of contemptuous authority*] Choke off dat noise! Where d'yuh get dat beer stuff? Beer, hell! Beer's for goils—and Dutchmen. Me for somep'n wit a kick to it! Gimme a drink, one of youse guys. [*Several bottles are eagerly offered. He takes a tremendous gulp at one of them; then, keeping the bottle in his hand, glares belligerently at the owner, who hastens to acquiesce in this robbery by saying*] All righto, Yank. Keep it and have another. [YANK *contemptuously turns his back on the crowd again. For a second there is an embarrassed silence. Then——*]

VOICES We must be passing the Hook.
    She's beginning to roll to it.
    Six days in hell—and then Southampton.
    Py Yesus, I vish somepody take my
        first vatch for me!
    Gittin' seasick, Square-head?
    Drink up and forget it!
    What's in your bottle?
    Gin.
    Dot's a nigger trink.
    Absinthe? It's doped. You'll go off
        your chump, Froggy!
    Cochon!
    Whisky, that's the ticket!
    Where's Paddy?
    Going asleep.
    Sing us that whisky song, Paddy.

[*They all turn to an old, wizened Irishman who is dozing, very drunk, on the benches forward. His face is extremely monkey-like with all the sad, patient pathos of that animal in his small eyes.*]

        Singa da song, Caruso Pat!
        He's gettin' old. The drink is too much for him.
        He's too drunk.

PADDY [*Blinking about him, starts to his feet resentfully, swaying, holding on to the edge of a bunk*] I'm never too drunk to sing. 'Tis only when I'm dead to the world I'd be wishful to sing at all. [*With a sort of sad contempt*] "Whisky Johnny," ye want? A chanty, ye want? Now that's a queer wish from the ugly like of you. God help you. But no mather, [*He starts to sing in a thin, nasal, doleful tone*]

"Oh, whisky is the life of man!
   Whisky! O Johnny! [*They all join in on this.*]
Oh, whisky is the life of man!
   Whisky for my Johnny! [*Again chorus.*]
Oh, whisky drove my old man mad!
   Whisky! O Johnny!
Oh, whisky drove my old man mad!
   Whisky for my Johnny!"

YANK [*Again turning around scornfully*] Aw hell! Nix on dat old sailing ship stuff! All dat bull's dead, see? And you're dead, too, yuh damned old Harp, on'y yuh don't know it. Take it easy, see. Give us a rest. Nix on de loud noise. [*With a cynical grin*] Can't youse see I'm tryin' to t'ink?

## 170   THE HAIRY APE

ALL [*Repeating the word after him as one with the same cynical amused mockery*] Think! [*The chorused word has a brazen metallic quality as if their throats were phonograph horns. It is followed by a general uproar of hard, barking laughter.*]

VOICES   Don't be cracking your head wit ut,
Yank.
You gat headache, py yingo!
One thing about it—it rhymes with
drink!
Ha, ha, ha!
Drink, don't think!
Drink, don't think!
Drink, don't think! [*A whole chorus of
voices has taken up this refrain,
stamping on the floor, pounding on
the benches with fists.*]

YANK [*Taking a gulp from his bottle—good-naturedly*] Aw right. Can de noise. I got yuh de foist time. [*The uproar subsides. A very drunken sentimental tenor begins to sing*]

"Far away in Canada,
   Far across the sea,
There's a lass who fondly waits
   Making a home for me——"

YANK [*Fiercely contemptuous*] Shut up, yuh lousy boob! Where d'yuh get dat tripe? Home? Home, hell! I'll make a home for yuh! I'll knock yuh dead. Home! T'hell wit home! Where d'yuh get dat tripe? Dis is home, see? What d'yuh want wit home? [*Proudly*] I runned away from mine when I was a kid. On'y too glad to beat it, dat was me. Home was lickings for me, dat's all. But yuh can bet your shoit no one ain't never licked me since! Wanter try it, any of youse? Huh! I guess not. [*In a more placated but still contemptuous tone*] Goils waitin' for yuh, huh? Aw, hell! Dat's all tripe. Dey don't wait for no one. Dey'd double-cross yuh for a nickel. Dey're all tarts, get me? Treat 'em rough, dat's me. To hell wit 'em. Tarts, dat's what, de whole bunch of 'em.

LONG [*Very drunk, jumps on a bench excitedly, gesticulating with a bottle in his hand*] Listen 'ere, Comrades. Yank 'ere is right. 'E says this 'ere stinkin' ship is our 'ome. And 'e says as 'ome is 'ell. And 'e's right! This is 'ell. We lives in 'ell, Comrades —and right enough we'll die in it. [*Raging*] And who's ter blame, I arsks yer? We ain't. We wasn't born this rotten way. All men is born free and ekal. That's in the bleedin' Bible, maties. But what d'they care for the Bible—them lazy, bloated swine what travels first cabin? Them's the ones. They dragged us down 'til we're on'y wage slaves in the bowels of a bloody ship, sweatin', burnin' up, eatin' coal dust! Hit's them's ter blame—the damned Capitalist clarss! [*There had been a gradual murmur of contemptuous resentment rising among the men until now he is interrupted by a storm of catcalls, hisses, boos, hard laughter.*]

VOICES  Turn it off!
Shut up!
Sit down!

Closa da face!

Tamn fool! [*Etc.*]

YANK [*Standing up and glaring at* LONG] Sit down before I knock yuh down! [LONG *makes haste to efface himself.* YANK *goes on contemptuously.*] De Bible, huh? De Cap'tlist class, huh? Aw nix on dat Salvation Army-Socialist bull. Git a soapbox! Hire a hall! Come and be saved, huh? Jerk us to Jesus, huh? Aw g'wan! I've listened to lots of guys like you, see. Yuh're all wrong. Wanter know what I t'ink? Yuh ain't no good for no one. Yuh're de bunk. Yuh ain't got no noive, get me? Yuh're yellow, dat's what. Yellow, dat's you. Say! What's dem slobs in de foist cabin got to do wit us? We're better men dan dey are, ain't we? Sure! One of us guys could clean up de whole mob wit one mit. Put one of 'em down here for one watch in de stokehole, what'd happen? Dey'd carry him off on a stretcher. Dem boids don't amount to nothin'. Dey're just baggage. Who makes dis old tub run? Ain't it us guys? Well den, we belong, don't we? We belong and dey don't. Dat's all. [*A loud chorus of approval.* YANK *goes on*] As for dis bein' hell—aw, nuts! Yuh lost your noive, dat's what. Dis is a man's job, get me? It belongs. It runs dis tub. No stiffs need apply. But yuh're a stiff, see? Yuh're yellow, dat's you.

VOICES [*With a great hard pride in them*]
Righto!
A man's job!
Talk is cheap, Long.
He never could hold up his end.
Divil take him!

## THE HAIRY APE 173

Yank's right. We make it go.
Py Gott, Yank say right ting!
We don't need no one cryin' over us.
Makin' speeches.
Throw him out!
Yellow!
Chuck him overboard!
I'll break his jaw for him!
[*They crowd around* LONG *threateningly.*]

YANK [*Half good-natured again—contemptuously*] Aw, take it easy. Leave him alone. He ain't woith a punch. Drink up. Here's how, whoever owns dis. [*He takes a long swallow from his bottle. All drink with him. In a flash all is hilarious amiability again, back-slapping, loud talk, etc.*]

PADDY [*Who has been sitting in a blinking, melancholy daze—suddenly cries out in a voice full of old sorrow*] We belong to this, you're saying? We make the ship to go, you're saying? Yerra then, that Almighty God have pity on us! [*His voice runs into the wail of a keen, he rocks back and forth on his bench. The men stare at him, startled and impressed in spite of themselves.*] Oh, to be back in the fine days of my youth, ochone! Oh, there was fine beautiful ships them days—clippers wid tall masts touching the sky—fine strong men in them—men that was sons of the sea as if 'twas the mother that bore them. Oh, the clean skins of them, and the clear eyes, the straight backs and full chests of them! Brave men they was, and bold men surely! We'd be sailing out, bound down round the Horn maybe.

We'd be making sail in the dawn, with a fair breeze, singing a chanty song wid no care to it. And astern the land would be sinking low and dying out, but we'd give it no heed but a laugh, and never a look behind. For the day that was, was enough, for we was free men—and I'm thinking 'tis only slaves do be giving heed to the day that's gone or the day to come—until they're old like me. [*With a sort of religious exaltation*] Oh, to be scudding south again wid the power of the Trade Wind driving her on steady through the nights and the days! Full sail on her! Nights and days! Nights when the foam of the wake would be flaming wid fire, when the sky'd be blazing and winking wid stars. Or the full of the moon maybe. Then you'd see her driving through the gray night, her sails stretching aloft all silver and white, not a sound on the deck, the lot of us dreaming dreams, till you'd believe 'twas no real ship at all you was on but a ghost ship like the *Flying Dutchman* they say does be roaming the seas forevermore widout touching a port. And there was the days, too. A warm sun on the clean decks. Sun warming the blood of you, and wind over the miles of shiny green ocean like strong drink to your lungs. Work—aye, hard work—but who'd mind that at all? Sure, you worked under the sky and 'twas work wid skill and daring to it. And wid the day done, in the dog watch, smoking me pipe at ease, the lookout would be raising land maybe, and we'd see the mountains of South Americy wid the red fire of the setting sun painting their white tops and the clouds floating by them! [*His tone of exaltation ceases. He goes on mournfully*] Yerra, what's the use of talking? 'Tis a dead man's whisper. [*To* YANK *resentfully*] 'Twas them days men belonged to ships, not now. 'Twas them days a ship was part of the sea, and a man was part of a ship, and the sea joined all together and made it one. [*Scornfully*] Is it one wid this you'd be, Yank—black smoke from the funnels smudging the sea, smudging the decks—the bloody engines pounding and throbbing and shaking—wid divil a sight of sun or a breath of clean air—choking our lungs wid coal dust—breaking our backs and hearts in the hell of the stokehole—feeding the bloody furnace—feeding our lives along wid the coal, I'm thinking—caged in by steel from a sight of the sky like bloody apes in the Zoo! [*With a harsh laugh*] Ho-ho, divil mend you! Is it to belong to that you're wishing? Is it a flesh and blood wheel of the engines you'd be?

YANK [*Who has been listening with a contemptuous sneer, barks out the answer*] Sure ting! Dat's me. What about it?

PADDY [*As if to himself—with great sorrow*] Me time is past due. That a great wave wid sun in the heart of it may sweep me over the side sometime I'd be dreaming of the days that's gone!

YANK  Aw, yuh crazy Mick! [*He springs to his feet and advances on Paddy threateningly—then stops, fighting some queer struggle within himself—lets his hands fall to his sides—contemptuously.*] Aw, take it easy. Yuh're aw right, at dat. Yuh're bugs, dat's all—nutty as a cuckoo. All dat tripe yuh been pullin' —Aw, dat's all right. On'y it's dead, get me? Yuh don't belong no more, see. Yuh don't get de stuff. Yuh're too old. [*Disgustedly*] But aw say, come up for air onct in a while, can't yuh? See what's happened since yuh croaked. [*He suddenly bursts forth vehemently, growing more and more excited.*] Say! Sure! Sure I meant it! What de hell—Say, lemme talk! Hey! Hey, you old Harp! Hey, youse guys! Say, listen to me—wait a moment—I gotta talk, see. I belong and he don't. He's dead but I'm livin'. Listen to me! Sure I'm part of de engines! Why de hell not? Dey move, don't dey? Dey're speed, ain't dey? Dey smash trou, don't dey? Twenty-five knots a hour! Dat's goin' some! Dat's new stuff! Dat belongs! But him, he's too old. He gets dizzy. Say, listen. All dat crazy tripe about nights and days; all dat crazy tripe about stars and moons; all dat crazy tripe about suns and winds, fresh air and de rest of it—Aw hell, dat's all a dope dream! Hittin' de pipe of de past, dat's what he's doin'. He's old and don't belong no more. But me, I'm young! I'm in de pink! I move wit it! It, get me! I mean de ting dat's de guts of all dis. It ploughs trou all de tripe he's been sayin'. It blows dat up! It knocks dat dead! It slams dat offen de face of de oith! It, get me! De engines and de coal and de smoke and all de rest of it! He can't breathe and swallow coal dust, but I kin, see? Dat's fresh air for me! Dat's food for me! I'm new, get me? Hell in de stokehole? Sure! It takes a man to work in hell. Hell, sure, dat's my fav'rite climate. I eat it up! I git fat on it! It's me makes it hot! It's me makes it roar! It's me makes it move! Sure, on'y for me everyting stops. It all goes dead, get me? De noise and smoke and all de engines movin' de woild, dey stop. Dere ain't nothin' no more! Dat's what I'm sayin'. Everyting else dat makes de woild move, somep'n makes it move. It can't move witout somep'n else, see? Den yuh get down to me. I'm at de bottom, get me! Dere ain't nothin' foither. I'm de end! I'm de start! I start somep'n and de woild moves! It—dat's me!—de new dat's moiderin' de old! I'm de ting in coal dat makes it boin; I'm steam and oil for de engines; I'm de ting in noise dat makes yuh hear it; I'm smoke and express trains and steamers and factory whistles; I'm de ting in gold dat makes money! And I'm what makes iron into steel! Steel, dat stands for de whole ting! And I'm steel—steel—steel! I'm de muscles in steel, de punch behind it. [*As he says this he pounds with his fist against the steel bunks. All the men, roused to a pitch of frenzied self-glorification by his speech, do likewise. There is a deafening metallic roar, through which* YANK's *voice can be heard bellowing.*] Slaves, hell! We run de whole woiks. All de rich guys dat tink dey're somep'n, dey ain't nothin'! Dey don't belong. But us guys, we're in de move, we're at de bottom, de whole ting is us! [PADDY *from the start of* YANK's *speech has been taking one gulp after another from his bottle, at first frightenedly, as if he were afraid to listen, then desperately, as if to drown his senses, but finally has achieved complete indifferent, even amused, drunkenness.* YANK *sees his lips moving. He quells the uproar with a shout.*] Hey, youse guys, take it easy! Wait a moment! De nutty Harp is sayin' somep'n.

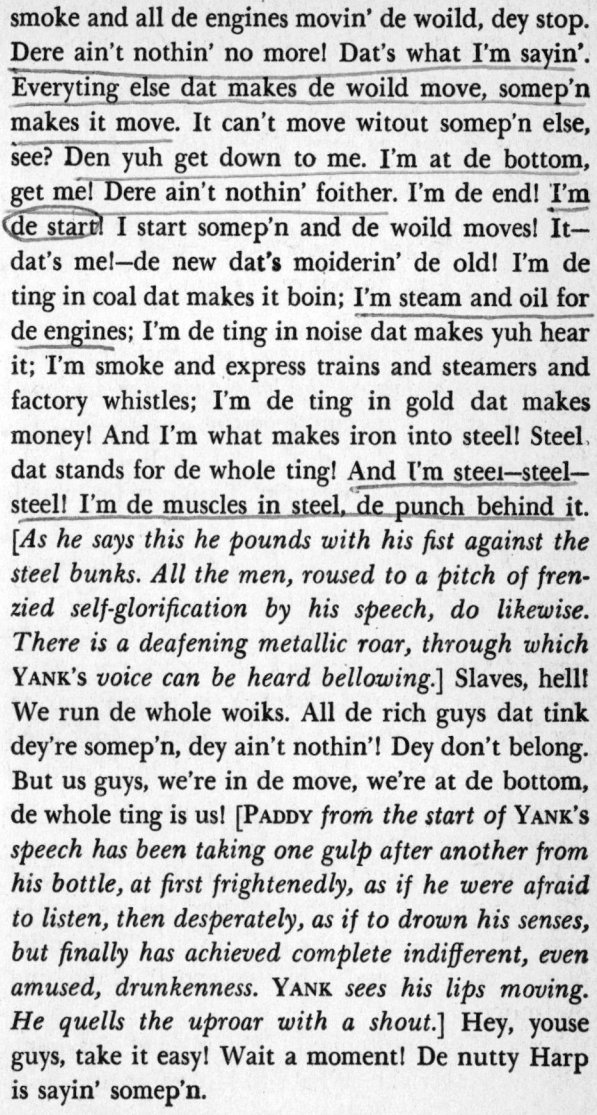

PADDY [*Is heard now—throws his head back with a mocking burst of laughter*]  Ho-ho-ho-ho-ho——

YANK [*Drawing back his fist, with a snarl*]  Aw! Look out who yuh're givin' the bark!

PADDY [*Begins to sing "The Miller of Dee" with enormous good nature*]

"I care for nobody, no, not I,
And nobody cares for me."

YANK [*Good-natured himself in a flash, interrupts* PADDY *with a slap on the bare back like a report*] Dat's de stuff! Now yuh're gettin' wise to somep'n. Care for nobody, dat's de dope! To hell wit 'em all! And nix on nobody else carin'. I kin care for myself, get me! [*Eight bells sound, muffled, vibrating through the steel walls as if some enormous brazen gong were imbedded in the heart of the ship. All the men jump up mechanically, file through the door silently close upon each other's heels in what is very like a prisoners' lockstep.* YANK *slaps* PADDY *on the back*]. Our watch, yuh old Harp! [*Mockingly*] Come on down in hell. Eat up de coal dust. Drink in de heat. It's it, see! Act like yuh like it, yuh better—or croak yuhself.

PADDY [*With jovial defiance*]  To the divil wid it! I'll not report this watch. Let thim log me and be damned. I'm no slave the like of you. I'll be sittin' here at me ease, and drinking, and thinking, and dreaming dreams.

YANK [*Contemptuousy*]  Tinkin' and dreamin', what'll that get yuh? What's tinkin' got to do wit it?

We move, don't we? Speed, ain't it? Fog, dat's all you stand for. But we drive trou dat, don't we? We split dat up and smash trou—twenty-five knots a hour! [*Turns his back on* PADDY *scornfully.*] Aw, yuh make me sick! Yuh don't belong! [*He strides out the door in rear. Paddy hums to himself, blinking drowsily.*]

[*The curtain falls.*]

# SCENE TWO

SCENE *Two days out. A section of the promenade deck.* MILDRED DOUGLAS *and her aunt are discovered reclining in deck chairs. The former is a girl of twenty, slender, delicate, with a pale, pretty face marred by a self-conscious expression of disdainful superiority. She looks fretful, nervous and discontented, bored by her own anemia. Her aunt is a pompous and proud—and fat—old lady. She is a type even to the point of a double chin and lorgnettes. She is dressed pretentiously, as if afraid her face alone would never indicate her position in life.* MILDRED *is dressed all in white.*

*The impression to be conveyed by this scene is one of the beautiful, vivid life of the sea all about—sunshine on the deck in a great flood, the fresh sea wind blowing across it. In the midst of this, these two incongruous, artificial figures, inert and disharmonious, the elder like a gray lump of dough touched up with rouge, the younger looking as if the vitality of her stock had been sapped before she was conceived, so that she is the expression not of its life energy but merely of the artificialities that energy had won for itself in the spending.*

MILDRED [*Looking up with affected dreaminess*] How the black smoke swirls back against the sky! Is it not beautiful?

AUNT [*Without looking up*] I dislike smoke of any kind.

MILDRED My great-grandmother smoked a pipe—a clay pipe.

AUNT [*Ruffling*] Vulgar!

MILDRED She was too distant a relative to be vulgar. Time mellows pipes.

AUNT [*Pretending boredom but irritated*] Did the sociology you took up at college teach you that—to play the ghoul on every possible occasion, excavating old bones? Why not let your great-grandmother rest in her grave?

MILDRED [*Dreamily*] With her pipe beside her—puffing in Paradise.

AUNT [*With spite*] Yes, you are a natural born ghoul. You are even getting to look like one, my dear.

MILDRED [*In a passionless tone*] I detest you, Aunt. [*Looking at her critically*] Do you know what you remind me of? Of a cold pork pudding against a background of linoleum tablecloth in the kitchen of a—but the possibilities are wearisome. [*She closes her eyes.*]

AUNT [*With a bitter laugh*] Merci for your candor. But since I am and must be your chaperon—in appearance—at least—let us patch up some sort of armed truce. For my part you are quite free to indulge any pose of eccentricity that beguiles you—as long as you observe the amenities——

MILDRED [*Drawling*] The inanities?

AUNT [*Going on as if she hadn't heard*] After exhausting the morbid thrills of social service work on New York's East Side—how they must have hated you, by the way, the poor that you made so much poorer in their own eyes!—you are now bent on making your slumming international. Well, I hope Whitechapel will provide the needed nerve tonic. Do not ask me to chaperon you there, however. I told your father I would not. I loathe deformity. We will hire an army of detectives and you may investigate everything—they allow you to see.

MILDRED [*Protesting with a trace of genuine earnestness*] Please do not mock at my attempts to discover how the other half lives. Give me credit for some sort of groping sincerity in that at least. I would like to help them. I would like to be of some use in the world. Is it my fault I don't know how? I would like to be sincere, to touch life somewhere. [*With weary bitterness*] But I'm afraid I have neither the vitality nor integrity. All that was burnt out in our stock before I was born. Grandfather's blast furnaces, flaming to the sky, melting steel, making millions—then father keeping those home fires burning, making more millions—and little me at the tail-end of it all. I'm a waste product in the Bessemer process—like the millions. Or rather, I inherit the acquired trait of the by-product, wealth, but none of the energy, none of the strength of the steel that made it. I am sired by gold and damned by it, as they say at the race track—damned in more ways than one. [*She laughs mirthlessly.*]

AUNT [*Unimpressed—superciliously*] You seem to be going in for sincerity today. It isn't becoming to you, really—except as an obvious pose. Be as artificial as you are, I advise. There's a sort of sincerity in that, you know. And, after all, you must confess you like that better.

MILDRED [*Again affected and bored*] Yes, I suppose I do. Pardon me for my outburst. When a leopard complains of its spots, it must sound rather grotesque. [*In a mocking tone*] Purr, little leopard. Purr, scratch, tear, kill, gorge yourself and be happy —only stay in the jungle, where your spots are camouflage. In a cage they make you conspicuous.

AUNT  I don't know what you are talking about.

MILDRED  It would be rude to talk about anything to you. Let's just talk. [*She looks at her wrist watch.*] Well, thank goodness, it's about time for them to come for me. That ought to give me a new thrill, Aunt.

AUNT [*Affectedly troubled*] You don't mean to say you're going? The dirt—the heat must be frightful——

MILDRED  Grandfather started as a puddler. I should have inherited an immunity to heat that would make a salamander shiver. It will be fun to put it to the test.

AUNT  But don't you have to have the captain's—or someone's—permission to visit the stokehole?

MILDRED [*With a triumphant smile*]  I have it—both his and the chief engineer's. Oh, they didn't want to at first, in spite of my social service credentials. They didn't seem a bit anxious that I should investigate how the other half lives and works on a ship. So I had to tell them that my father, the president of Nazareth Steel, chairman of the board of directors of this line, had told me it would be all right

AUNT  He didn't.

MILDRED  How naïve age makes one! But I said he did, Aunt. I even said he had given me a letter to them—which I had lost. And they were afraid to take the chance that I might be lying. [*Excitedly*] So it's ho! for the stokehole. The second engineer is to escort me. [*Looking at her watch again.*] It's time. And here he comes, I think. [*The* SECOND ENGINEER *enters. He is a husky, fine-looking man of thirty-five or so. He stops before the two and tips his cap, visibly embarrassed and ill-at-ease.*]

SECOND ENGINEER  Miss Douglas?

MILDRED  Yes. [*Throwing off her rugs and getting to her feet*] Are we all ready to start?

SECONE ENGINEER  In just a second, ma'am. I'm waiting for the Fourth. He's coming along.

MILDRED [*With a scornful smile*]  You don't care to shoulder this responsibility alone, is that it?

SECOND ENGINEER [*Forcing a smile*] Two are better than one. [*Disturbed by her eyes, glances out to sea—blurts out*] A fine day we're having.

MILDRED  Is it?

SECOND ENGINEER  A nice warm breeze——

MILDRED  It feels cold to me.

SECOND ENGINEER  But it's hot enough in the sun——

MILDRED  Not hot enough for me. I don't like Nature. I was never athletic.

SECOND ENGINEER [*Forcing a smile*] Well, you'll find it hot enough where you're going.

MILDRED  Do you mean hell?

SECOND ENGINEER [*Flabbergasted, decides to laugh*] Ho-ho! No, I mean the stokehole.

MILDRED  My grandfather was a puddler. He played with boiling steel.

SECOND ENGINEER [*All at sea—uneasily*] Is that so? Hum, you'll excuse me, ma'am, but are you intending to wear that dress?

MILDRED  Why not?

SECOND ENGINEER  You'll likely rub against oil and dirt. It can't be helped.

MILDRED  It doesn't matter. I have lots of white dresses.

SECOND ENGINEER  I have an old coat you might throw over——

MILDRED  I have fifty dresses like this. I will throw this one into the sea when I come back. That ought to wash it clean, don't you think?

SECOND ENGINEER [*Doggedly*] There's ladders to

climb down that are none too clean—and dark alleyways——

MILDRED  I will wear this very dress and none other.

SECOND ENGINEER  No offense meant. It's none of my business. I was only warning you——

MILDRED  Warning? That sounds thrilling.

SECOND ENGINEER [*Looking down the deck—with a sigh of relief*]  There's the Fourth now. He's waiting for us. If you'll come——

MILDRED  Go on. I'll follow you. [*He goes.* MILDRED *turns a mocking smile on her aunt.*] An oaf—but a handsome, virile oaf.

AUNT [*Scornfully*]  Poser!

MILDRED  Take care. He said there were dark alleyways——

AUNT [*In the same tone*]  Poser!

MILDRED [*Biting her lips angrily*]  You are right. But would that my millions were not so anemically chaste!

AUNT  Yes, for a fresh pose I have no doubt you would drag the name of Douglas in the gutter!

MILDRED  From which it sprang. Good-by, Aunt. Don't pray too hard that I may fall into the fiery furnace.

AUNT  Poser!

MILDRED [*Viciously*]  Old hag! [*She slaps her aunt insultingly across the face and walks off, laughing gaily.*]

AUNT [*Screams after her*]  I said poser!

[*The curtain falls.*]

# SCENE THREE

SCENE *The stokehole. In the rear, the dimly-outlined bulks of the furnaces and boilers. High overhead one hanging electric bulb sheds just enough light through the murky air laden with coal dust to pile up masses of shadows everywhere. A line of men, stripped to the waist, is before the furnace doors. They bend over, looking neither to right nor left, handling their shovels as if they were part of their bodies, with a strange, awkward, swinging rhythm. They use the shovels to throw open the furnace doors. Then from these fiery round holes in the black a flood of terrific light and heat pours full upon the men who are outlined in silhouette in the crouching, inhuman attitudes of chained gorillas. The men shovel with a rhythmic motion, swinging as on a pivot from the coal which lies in heaps on the floor behind to hurl it into the flaming mouths before them. There is a tumult of noise—the brazen clang of the furnace doors as they are flung open or slammed shut, the grating, teeth-gritting grind of steel against steel, of crunching coal. This clash of sounds stuns one's ears with its rending dissonance. But there is order in it, rhythm, a mechanical regulated recurrence, a tempo. And rising above all, making the air hum with the quiver of liberated energy, the roar of leaping flames in the furnaces, the monotonous throbbing beat of the engines.*

*As the curtain rises, the furnace doors are shut. The men are taking a breathing spell. One or two are arranging the coal behind them, pulling it into more accessible heaps. The others can be dimly made out leaning on their shovels in relaxed attitudes of exhaustion.*

PADDY [*From somewhere in the line—plaintively*] Yerra, will this divil's own watch nivir end? Me back is broke. I'm destroyed entirely.

YANK [*From the center of the line—with exuberant scorn*] Aw, yuh make me sick! Lie down and croak, why don't yuh? Always beefin', dat's you! Say, dis is a cinch! Dis was made for me! It's my meat, get me! [*A whistle is blown—a thin, shrill note from somewhere overhead in the darkness.* YANK *curses without resentment.*] Dere's de damn engineer crackin' de whip. He tinks we're loafin'.

PADDY [*Vindictively*] God stiffen him!

YANK [*In an exultant tone of command*] Come

on, youse guys! Git into de game! She's gettin' hungry! Pile some grub in her. Trow it into her belly! Come on now, all of youse! Open her up! [*At this last all the men, who have followed his movements of getting into position, throw open their furnace doors with a deafening clang. The fiery light floods over their shoulders as they bend round for the coal. Rivulets of sooty sweat have traced maps on their backs. The enlarged muscles form bunches of high light and shadow.*]

YANK [*Chanting a count as he shovels without seeming effort*] One—two—tree—— [*His voice rising exultantly in the joy of battle*] Dat's de stuff! Let her have it! All togedder now! Sling it into her! Let her ride! Shoot de piece now! Call de toin on her! Drive her into it! Feel her move. Watch her smoke! Speed, dat's her middle name! Give her coal, youse guys! Coal, dat's her booze! Drink it up, baby! Let's see yuh sprint! Dig in and gain a lap! Dere she go-o-es. [*This last in the chanting formula of the galley gods at the six-day bike race. He slams his furnace door shut. The others do likewise with as much unison as their wearied bodies will permit The effect is of one fiery eye after another being blotted out with a series of accompanying bangs.*]

PADDY [*Groaning*] Me back is broke. I'm bate out—bate— [*There is a pause. Then the inexorable whistle sounds again from the dim regions above the electric light. There is a growl of cursing rage from all sides.*]

YANK [*Shaking his fist upward—contemptuously*]

Take it easy dere, you! Who d'yuh tinks runnin' dis game, me or you? When I git ready, we move. Not before! When I git ready, get me!

VOICES [*Approvingly*]
> That's the stuff!
> Yank tal him, py golly!
> Yank ain't afeerd.
> Goot poy, Yank!
> Give him hell!
> Tell 'im 'e's a bloody swine!
> Bloody slave-driver!

YANK [*Contemptuously*] He ain't got no noive. He's yellow, get me? All de engineers is yellow. Dey got streaks a mile wide. Aw, to hell with him! Let's move, youse guys. We had a rest. Come on, she needs it! Give her pep! It ain't for him. Him and his whistle, dey don't belong. But we belong, see! We gotter feed de baby! Come on! [*He turns and flings his furnace door open. They all follow his lead. At this instant the* SECOND *and* FOURTH EN-GINEERS *enter from the darkness on the left with* MILDRED *between them. She starts, turns paler, her pose is crumbling, she shivers with fright in spite of the blazing heat, but forces herself to leave the* EN-GINEERS *and take a few steps near the men. She is right behind* YANK. *All this happens quickly while the men have their backs turned.*]

YANK Come on, youse guys! [*He is turning to get coal when the whistle sounds again in a peremptory, irritating note. This drives* YANK *into a sudden fury. While the other men have turned full around and stopped dumbfounded by the spectacle of* MILDRED *standing there in her white dress,* YANK *does not turn far enough to see her. Besides, his head is thrown back, he blinks upward through the murk trying to find the owner of the whistle, he brandishes his shovel murderously over his head in one hand, pounding on his chest, gorilla-like, with the other, shouting.*] Toin off dat whistle! Come down outa dere, yuh yellow, brass-buttoned, Belfast bum, yuh! Come down and I'll knock yer brains out! Yuh lousy, stinkin, yellow mut of a Catholic-moiderin' bastard! Come down and I'll moider yuh! Pullin' dat whistle on me, huh? I'll show yuh! I'll crash yer skull in! I'll drive yer teet' down yer troat! I'll slam yer nose trou de back of yer head! I'll cut yer guts out for a nickel, yuh lousy boob, yuh dirty, crummy, muck-eatin' son of a—— [*Suddenly he becomes conscious of all the other men staring at something directly behind his back. He whirls defensively with a snarling, murderous growl, crouching to spring, his lips drawn back over his teeth, his small eyes gleaming ferociously. He sees* MILDRED, *like a white apparition in the full light from the open furnace doors. He glares into her eyes, turned to stone. As for her, during his speech she has listened, paralyzed with horror, terror, her whole personality crushed, beaten in, collapsed, by the terrific impact of this unknown, abysmal brutality, naked and shameless. As she looks at his gorilla face, as his eyes bore into hers, she utters a low, choking cry and shrinks away from him, putting both hands up be-*

## 192   THE HAIRY APE

*fore her eyes to shut out the sight of his face, to protect her own. This startles* YANK *to a reaction. His mouth falls open, his eyes grow bewildered.*]

MILDRED [*About to faint—to the* ENGINEERS, *who now have her one by each arm—whimperingly*] Take me away! Oh, the filthy beast! [*She faints. They carry her quickly back, disappearing in the darkness at the left, rear. An iron door clangs shut. Rage and bewildered fury rush back on* YANK. *He feels himself insulted in some unknown fashion in the very heart of his pride. He roars.*] God damn yuh! [*And hurls his shovel after them at the door which has just closed. It hits the steel bulkhead with a clang and falls clattering on the steel floor. From overhead the whistle sounds again in a long, angry, insistent command.*]

[*The curtain falls.*]

# SCENE FOUR

SCENE *The firemen's forecastle. YANK's watch has just come off duty and had dinner. Their faces and bodies shine from a soap and water scrubbing but around their eyes, where a hasty dousing does not touch, the coal dust sticks like black make-up, giving them a queer, sinister expression. YANK has not washed either face or body. He stands out in contrast to them, a blackened, brooding figure. He is seated forward on a bench in the exact attitude of Rodin's "The Thinker." The others, most of them smoking pipes, are staring at YANK half-apprehensively, as if fearing an outburst; half-amusedly, as if they saw a joke somewhere that tickled them.*

VOICES   He ain't ate nothin'.
        Py golly, a fallar gat to gat grub in him.
        Divil a lie.
        Yank feeda da fire, no feeda da face.
        Ha-ha.

## THE HAIRY APE

He ain't even washed hisself.

He's forgot.

Hey, Yank, you forgot to wash.

YANK [*Sullenly*] Forgot nothin'! To hell wit washin'.

VOICES  It'll stick to you.

It'll get under your skin.

Give yer the bleedin' itch, that's wot.

It makes spots on you—like a leopard.

Like a piebald nigger, you mean.

Better wash up, Yank.

You sleep better.

Wash up, Yank.

Wash up! Wash up!

YANK [*Resentfully*] Aw say, youse guys. Lemme alone. Can't youse see I'm tryin' to tink?

ALL [*Repeating the word after him as one with cynical mockery*] Think! [*The word has a brazen, metallic quality as if their throats were phonograph horns. It is followed by a chorus of hard, barking laughter.*]

YANK [*Springing to his feet and glaring at them belligerently*] Yes, tink! Tink, dat's what I said! What about it? [*They are silent, puzzled by his sudden resentment at what used to be one of his jokes.* YANK *sits down again in the same attitude of "The Thinker."*]

VOICES  Leave him alone.

He's got a grouch on.

Why wouldn't he?

PADDY [*With a wink at the others*] Sure I know

what's the matther. 'Tis aisy to see. He's fallen in love, I'm telling you.

ALL [*Repeating the word after him as one with cynical mockery*] Love! [*The word has a brazen, metallic quality as if their throats were phonograph horns. It is followed by a chorus of hard, barking laughter.*]

YANK [*With a contemptuous snort*] Love, hell! Hate, dat's what. I've fallen in hate, get me?

PADDY [*Philosophically*] 'Twould take a wise man to tell one from the other. [*With a bitter, ironical scorn, increasing as he goes on.*] But I'm telling you it's love that's in it. Sure what else but love for us poor bastes in the stokehole would be bringing a fine lady, dressed like a white quane, down a mile of ladders and steps to be havin' a look at us? [*A growl of anger goes up from all sides.*]

LONG [*Jumping on a bench—hecticly*] Hinsultin' us! Hinsultin' us, the bloody cow! And them bloody engineers! What right 'as they got to be exhibitin' us 's if we was bleedin' monkeys in a menagerie? Did we sign for hinsults to our dignity as 'onest workers? Is that in the ship's articles? You kin bloody well bet it ain't! But I knows why they done it. I arsked a deck steward 'o she was and 'e told me. 'Er old man's a bleedin' millionaire, a bloody Capitalist! 'E's got enuf bloody gold to sink this bleedin' ship! 'E makes arf the bloody steel in the world! 'E owns this bloody boat! And you and me, Comrades, we're 'is slaves! And the skipper and mates and engineers, they're 'is slaves! And she's 'is bloody daughter and we're all 'er slaves, too! And she gives 'er orders as 'ow she wants to see the bloody animals below decks and down they take 'er! [*There is a roar of rage from all sides.*]

YANK [*Blinking at him bewilderedly*] Say! Wait a moment! Is all dat straight goods?

LONG Straight as string! The bleedin' steward as waits on 'em, 'e told me about 'er. And what're we goin' ter do, I arsks yer? 'Ave we got ter swaller 'er hinsults like dogs? It ain't in the ship's articles. I tell yer we got a case. We kin go to law——

YANK [*With abysmal contempt*] Hell! Law!

ALL [*Repeating the word after him as one with cynical mockery*] Law! [*The word has a brazen metallic quality as if their throats were phonograph horns. It is followed by a chorus of hard, barking laughter.*]

LONG [*Feeling the ground slipping from under his feet—desperately*] As voters and citizens we kin force the bloody governments——

YANK [*With abysmal contempt*] Hell! Governments!

ALL [*Repeating the word after him as one with cynical mockery*] Governments! [*The word has a brazen metallic quality as if their throats were phonograph horns. It is followed by a chorus of hard, barking laughter.*]

LONG [*Hysterically*] We're free and equal in the sight of God——

YANK [*With abysmal contempt*] Hell! God!

ALL [*Repeating the word after him as one with cynical mockery*] God! [*The word has a brazen *metallic quality as if their throats were phonograph horns. It is followed by a chorus of hard, barking, laughter.*]

YANK [*Witheringly*] Aw, join de Salvation Army!

ALL  Sit down! Shut up! Damn fool! Sea-lawyer! [LONG *slinks back out of sight.*]

PADDY [*Continuing the trend of his thoughts as if he had never been interrupted—bitterly*] And there she was standing behind us, and the Second pointing at us like a man you'd hear in a circus would be saying: In this cage is a queerer kind of baboon than ever you'd find in darkest Africy. We roast them in their own sweat—and be damned if you won't hear some of thim saying they like it! [*He glances scornfully at* YANK.]

YANK [*With a bewildered uncertain growl*] Aw!

PADDY  And there was Yank roarin' curses and turning round wid his shovel to brain her—and she looked at him, and him at her——

YANK [*Slowly*] She was all white. I thought she was a ghost. Sure.

PADDY [*With heavy, biting sarcasm*] 'Twas love at first sight, divil a doubt of it! If you'd seen the endearin' look on her pale mug when she shriveled away with her hands over her eyes to shut out the sight of him! Sure, 'twas as if she'd seen a great hairy ape escaped from the Zoo!

YANK [*Stung—with a growl of rage*] Aw!

PADDY  And the loving way Yank heaved his shovel at the skull of her, only she was out the door! [*A grin breaking over his face*] 'Twas touching, I'm telling you! It put the touch of home, swate home in the stokehole. [*There is a roar of laughter from all.*]

YANK [*Glaring at* PADDY *menacingly*] Aw, choke dat off, see!

PADDY [*Not heeding him—to the others*] And her grabbin' at the Second's arm for protection. [*With a grotesque imitation of a woman's voice*] Kiss me, Engineer dear, for it's dark down here and me old man's in Wall Street making money! Hug me tight, darlin', for I'm afeerd in the dark and me mother's on deck makin' eyes at the skipper! [*Another roar of laughter*]

YANK [*Threateningly*] Say! What yuh tryin' to do, kid me, yuh old Harp?

PADDY Divil a bit! Ain't I wishin' myself you'd brained her?

YANK [*Fiercely*] I'll brain her! I'll brain her yet, wait 'n' see! [*Coming over to* PADDY *slowly*] Say, is dat what she called me—a hairy ape?

PADDY She looked it at you if she didn't say the word itself.

YANK [*Grinning horribly*] Hairy ape, huh? Sure! Dat's de way she looked at me, aw right. Hairy ape! So dat's me, huh? [*Bursting into rage—as if she were still in front of him*] Yuh skinny tart! Yuh white-faced bum, yuh! I'll show yuh who's a ape! [*Turning to the others, bewilderment seizing him again*] Say, youse guys. I was bawlin' him out for pullin' de whistle on us. You heard me. And den I seen youse lookin' at somep'n and I tought he'd sneaked down to come up in back of me, and I hopped round to knock him dead wit de shovel. And dere she was wit de light on her! Christ, yuh coulda pushed me over with a finger! I was scared, get me? Sure! I tought she was a ghost, see? She was all in white like dey wrap around stiffs. You seen her. Kin yuh blame me? She didn't belong, dat's what. And den when I come to and seen it was a real skoit and seen de way she was lookin' at me—like Paddy said—Christ, I was sore, get me? I don't stand for dat stuff from nobody. And I flung de shovel—on'y she'd beat it. [*Furiously*] I wished it'd banged her! I wished it'd knocked her block off!

LONG And be 'anged for murder or 'lectrocuted? She ain't bleedin' well worth it.

YANK I don't give a damn what! I'd be square wit her, wouldn't I? Tink I wanter let her put somep'n over on me? Tink I'm goin' to let her git away wit dat stuff? Yuh don't know me! No one ain't never put nothin' over on me and got away wit it, see!—not dat kind of stuff—no guy and no skoit neither! I'll fix her! Maybe she'll come down again——

VOICE No chance, Yank. You scared her out of a year's growth.

YANK I scared her? Why de hell should I scare her? Who de hell is she? Ain't she de same as me? Hairy ape, huh? [*With his old confident bravado*] I'll show her I'm better'n her, if she on'y knew it. I belong and she don't, see! I move and she's dead! Twenty-five knots a hour, dat's me! Dat carries her but I make dat. She's on'y baggage. Sure! [*Again bewilderedly*] But, Christ, she was funny lookin'!

Did yuh pipe her hands? White and skinny. Yuh could see de bones through 'em. And her mush, dat was dead white, too. And her eyes, dey was like dey'd seen a ghost. Me, dat was! Sure! Hairy ape! Ghost, huh? Look at dat arm! [*He extends his right arm, swelling out the great muscles.*] I coulda took her wit dat, wit' just my little finger even, and broke her in two. [*Again bewilderedly*] Say, who is dat skoit, huh? What is she? What's she come from? Who made her? Who give her de noive to look at me like dat? Dis ting's got my goat right. I don't get her. She's new to me. What does a skoit like her mean, huh? She don't belong, get me! I can't see her. [*With growing anger*] But one ting I'm wise to, aw right, aw right! Youse all kin bet your shoits I'll git even wit her. I'll show her if she tinks she—She grinds de organ and I'm on de string, huh? I'll fix her! Let her come down again and I'll fling her in de furnace! She'll move den! She won't shiver at nothin' den! Speed, dat'll be her! She'll belong den! [*He grins horribly.*]

PADDY  She'll never come. She's had her bellyfull, I'm telling you. She'll be in bed now, I'm thinking, wid ten doctors and nurses feedin' her salts to clean the fear out of her.

YANK [*Enraged*]  Yuh tink I made her sick, too, do yuh? Just lookin' at me, huh? Hairy ape, huh? [*In a frenzy of rage*] I'll fix her! I'll tell her where to git off! She'll git down on her knees and take it back or I'll bust de face offen her! [*Shaking one fist upward and beating on his chest with the other*] I'll find yuh! I'm comin', d'yuh hear? I'll fix yuh, God damn yuh! [*He makes a rush for the door.*]

VOICES   Stop him!
He'll get shot!
He'll murder her!
Trip him up!
Hold him!
He's gone crazy!
Gott, he's strong!
Hold him down!
Look out for a kick!
Pin his arms!

[*They have all piled on him and, after a fierce struggle, by sheer weight of numbers have borne him to the floor just inside the door.*]

PADDY [*Who has remained detached*] Kape him down till he's cooled off. [*Scornfully*] Yerra, Yank, you're a great fool. Is it payin' attention at all you are to the like of that skinny sow widout one drop of rale blood in her?

YANK [*Frenziedly, from the bottom of the heap*] She's done me doit! She done me doit, didn't she? I'll git square wit her! I'll get her some way! Git offen me, youse guys! Lemme up! I'll show her who's a ape!

[*The curtain falls.*]

# SCENE FIVE

SCENE *Three weeks later. A corner of Fifth Avenue in the Fifties on a fine Sunday morning. A general atmosphere of clean, well-tidied, wide street; a flood of mellow, tempered sunshine; gentle, genteel breezes. In the rear, the show windows of two shops, a jewelry establishment on the corner, a furrier's next to it. Here the adornments of extreme wealth are tantalizingly displayed. The jeweler's window is gaudy with glittering diamonds, emeralds, rubies, pearls, etc., fashioned in ornate tiaras, crowns, necklaces, collars, etc. From each piece hangs an enormous tag from which a dollar sign and numerals in intermittent electric lights wink out the incredible prices. The same in the furrier's. Rich furs of all varieties hang there bathed in a downpour of artificial light. The general effect is of a background of magnificence cheapened and made grotesque by commercialism, a background in tawdry disharmony with the clear light and sunshine on the street itself.*

*Up the side street* YANK *and* LONG *come swaggering.* LONG *is dressed in shore clothes, wears a black Windsor tie, cloth cap.* YANK *is in his dirty dungarees. A fireman's cap with black peak is cocked defiantly on the side of his head. He has not shaved for days and around his fierce, resentful eyes—as around those of* LONG *to a lesser degree—the black smudge of coal dust still sticks like make-up. They hesitate and stand together at the corner, swaggering, looking about them with a forced, defiant contempt.*

LONG [*Indicating it all with an oratorical gesture*] Well, 'ere we are. Fif' Avenoo. This 'ere's their bleedin' private lane, as yer might say. [*Bitterly*] We're trespassers 'ere. Proletarians keep orf the grass!

YANK [*Dully*] I don't see no grass, yuh boob. [*Staring at the sidewalk*] Clean, ain't it? Yuh could eat a fried egg offen it. The white wings got some job sweepin' dis up. [*Looking up and down the avenue—surlily*] Where's all de white-collar stiffs yuh said was here—and de skoits—*her* kind?

LONG In church, blarst 'em! Arskin' Jesus to give 'em more money.

YANK Choich, huh? I useter go to choich onct—sure—when I was a kid. Me old man and woman, dey made me. Dey never went demselves, dough. Always got too big a head on Sunday mornin', dat was dem. [*With a grin*] Dey was scrappers for fair, bot' of dem. On Satiday nights when dey bot' got a skinful dey could put up a bout oughter been staged at de Garden. When dey got trough dere wasn't a chair or table with a leg under it. Or else dey bot' jumped on me for somep'n. Dat was where I loined to take punishment. [*With a grin and a swagger*] I'm a chip offen de old block, get me?

LONG   Did yer old man follow the sea?

YANK   Naw. Worked along shore. I runned away when me old lady croaked with de tremens. I helped at truckin' and in de market. Den I shipped in de stokehole. Sure. Dat belongs. De rest was nothin'. [*Looking around him*] I ain't never seen dis before. De Brooklyn waterfront, dat was where I was dragged up. [*Taking a deep breath*] Dis ain't so bad at dat, huh?

LONG   Not bad? Well, we pays for it wiv our bloody sweat, if yer wants to know!

YANK   [*With sudden angry disgust*]   Aw, hell! I don't see no one, see—like her. All dis gives me a pain. It don't belong. Say, ain't dere a back room around dis dump? Let's go shoot a ball. All dis is too clean and quiet and dolled-up, get me? It gives me a pain.

LONG   Wait and yer'll bloody well see——

YANK   I don't wait for no one. I keep on de move. Say, what yuh drag me up here for, anyway? Tryin' to kid me, yuh simp, yuh?

LONG   Yer wants to get back at 'er, don't yer? That's what yer been sayin' every bloomin' hour since she hinsulted yer.

YANK   [*Vehemently*]   Sure ting I do! Didn't I try to get even wit her in Southampton? Didn't I sneak on de dock and wait for her by de gangplank? I was goin' to spit in her pale mug, see! Sure, right in her pop-eyes! Dat woulda made me even, see? But no chanct. Dere was a whole army of plainclothes bulls around. Dey spotted me and gimme de bum's rush. I never seen her. But I'll git square wit her yet, you watch! [*Furiously*] De lousy tart! She tink she kin get away with moider—but not wit me! I'll fix her! I'll tink of a way!

LONG [*As disgusted as he dares to be*] Ain't that why I brought yer up 'ere—to show yer? Yer been lookin' at this 'ere 'ole affair wrong. Yer been actin' an' talkin' 's if it was all a bleedin' personal matter between yer and that bloody cow. I wants to convince yer she was on'y a representative of 'er clarss. I wants to awaken yer bloody clarss consciousness. Then yer'll see it's 'er clarss yer've got to fight, not 'er alone. There's a 'ole mob of 'em like 'er, Gawd blind 'em!

YANK [*Spitting on his hands—belligerently*] De more de merrier when I gits started. Bring on de gang!

LONG Yer'll see 'em in arf a mo', when that church lets out. [*He turns and sees the window display in the two stores for the first time.*] Blimey! Look at that, will yer? [*They both walk back and stand looking in the jeweler's.* LONG *flies into a fury.*] Just look at this 'ere bloomin' mess! Just look at it! Look at the bleedin' prices on 'em—more'n our 'ole bloody stokehole makes in ten voyages sweatin' in 'ell! And they—'er and 'er bloody clarss—buys 'em

for toys to dangle on 'em! One of these 'ere, would
buy scoff for a starvin' family for a year!

YANK   Aw, cut de sob stuff! T' hell wit de starvin'
family! Yuh'll be passin' de hat to me next. [*With
naïve admiration*] Say, dem tings is pretty, huh?
Bet yuh dey'd hock for a piece of change aw right.
[*Then turning away, bored.*] But aw hell, what good
are dey? Let 'er have 'em. Dey don't belong no
more'n she does. [*With a gesture of sweeping the
jewelers into oblivion*] All dat don't count, get me?

LONG   [*Who has moved to the furrier's—indignantly*]   And I s'pose this 'ere don't count neither
—skins of poor, 'armless animals slaughtered so as
'er and 'ers can keep their bleedin' noses warm!

YANK   [*Who has been staring at something inside
—with queer excitement*]   Take a slant at dat! Give
it de once-over! Monkey fur—two t'ousand bucks!
[*Bewilderedly*] Is dat straight goods—monkey fur?
What de hell——?

LONG   [*Bitterly*]   It's straight enuf. [*With grim
humor*] They wouldn't bloody well pay that for
'airy ape's skin—no, nor for the 'ole livin' ape with
all 'is 'ead, and body, and soul thrown in!

YANK   [*Clenching his fists, his face growing pale
with rage as if the skin in the window were a personal insult*]   Trowin' it up in my face! Christ! I'll
fix her!

LONG   [*Excitedly*]   Church is out. 'Ere they come,
the bleedin' swine. [*After a glance at* YANK's *lowering face—uneasily*] Easy goes, Comrade. Keep yer
bloomin' temper. Remember force defeats itself. It
ain't our weapon. We must impress our demands

through peaceful means—the votes of the on-marching proletarians of the bloody world!

YANK [*With abysmal contempt*] Votes, hell! Votes is a joke, see. Votes for women! Let dem do it!

LONG [*Still more uneasily*] Calm, now. Treat 'em wiv the proper contempt. Observe the bleedin' parasites but 'old yer 'orses.

YANK [*Angrily*] Git away from me! Yuh're yellow, dat's what. Force, dat's me! De punch, dat's me every time, see! [*The crowd from church enter from the right, sauntering slowly and affectedly, their heads held stiffly up, looking neither to right nor left, talking in toneless, simpering voices. The women are rouged, calcimined, dyed, overdressed to the nth degree. The men are in Prince Alberts, high hats, spats, canes, etc. A procession of gaudy marionettes, yet with something of the relentless horror of Frankenstein monsters in their detached, mechanical unawareness.*]

VOICES Dear Doctor Caiaphas! He is so sincere!
What was the sermon? I dozed off.
About the radicals, my dear—and the false doctrines that are being preached.
We must organize a hundred per cent American bazaar.
And let everyone contribute one one-hundredth per cent of their income tax.
What an original idea!
We can devote the proceeds to rehabilitating the veil of the temple.
But that has been done so many times.

YANK [*Glaring from one to the other of them—with an insulting snort of scorn*] Huh! Huh! [*Without seeming to see him, they make wide detours to avoid the spot where he stands in the middle of the sidewalk.*]

LONG [*Frightenedly*] Keep yer bloomin' mouth shut, I tells yer.

YANK [*Viciously*] G'wan! Tell it to Sweeney! [*He swaggers away and deliberately lurches into a top-hatted gentleman, then glares at him pugnaciously.*] Say, who d'yuh tink yuh're bumpin'? Tink yuh own de oith?

GENTLEMAN [*Coldly and affectedly*] I beg your pardon. [*He has not looked at* YANK *and passes on without a glance, leaving him bewildered.*]

LONG [*Rushing up and grabbing* YANK'S *arm*] 'Ere! Come away! This wasn't what I meant. Yer'll 'ave the bloody coppers down on us.

YANK [*Savagely—giving him a push that sends him sprawling*] G'wan!

LONG [*Picks himself up—hysterically*] I'll pop orf then. This ain't what I meant. And whatever 'appens yer can't blame me. [*He slinks off left.*]

YANK T' hell wit youse! [*He approaches a lady —with a vicious grin and a smirking wink.*] Hello, Kiddo. How's every little ting? Got anyting on for tonight? I know an old boiler down to de docks we kin crawl into. [*The lady stalks by without a look, without a change of pace.* YANK *turns to others—insultingly.*] Holy smokes, what a mug! Go hide yuhself before de horses shy at yuh. Gee, pipe de heine on dat one! Say, youse, yuh look like de stoin of a ferryboat. Paint and powder! All dolled up to kill! Yuh look like stiffs laid out for de boneyard! Aw, g'wan, de lot of youse! Yuh give me de eye-ache. Yuh don't belong, get me! Look at me, why don't youse dare? I belong, dat's me! [*Pointing to skyscraper across the street which is in process of construction—with bravado*] See dat building goin' up dere? See de steel work? Steel, dat's me! Youse guys live on it and tink yuh're somep'n. But I'm *in* it, see! I'm de-hoistin' engine dat makes it go up! I'm it—de inside and bottom of it! Sure! I'm steel and steam and smoke and de rest of it! It moves— speed—twenty-five stories up—and me at de top and bottom—movin'! Youse simps don't move. Yuh're on'y dolls I winds up to see 'm spin. Yuh're de gar- bage, get me—de leavins—der ashes we dump over de side! Now, what's 'a' yuh gotta say? [*But as they seem neither to see nor hear him, he flies into a fury.*] Bums! Pigs! Tarts! Bitches! [*He turns in rage on the men, bumping viciously into them but not jarring them the least bit. Rather it is he who recoils after each collision. He keeps growling.*] Git off de oith! G'wan, yuh bum! Look where yuh're goin', can't yuh? Git outa here! Fight, why don't yuh? Put up yer mits! Don't be a dog! Fight or I'll knock yuh dead! [*But, without seeming to see him, they all answer with mechanical affected politeness.*] I beg your pardon. [*Then at a cry from one of the women they all scurry to the furrier's window.*]

THE WOMAN [*Ecstatically, with a gasp of delight*]

Monkey fur! [*The whole crowd of men and women chorus after her in the same tone of affected delight.*] Monkey fur!

YANK [*With a jerk of his head back on his shoulders, as if he had received a punch full in the face—raging*] I see yuh, all in white! I see yuh, yuh white-faced tart, yuh! Hairy ape, huh? I'll hairy ape yuh! [*He bends down and grips at the street curbing as if to pluck it out and hurl it. Foiled in this, snarling with passion, he leaps to the lamppost on the corner and tries to pull it up for a club. Just at that moment a bus is heard rumbling up. A fat, high-hatted, spatted gentleman runs out from the side street. He calls out plaintively.*] Bus! Bus! Stop there! [*And runs full tilt into the bending straining* YANK, *who is bowled off his balance.*]

YANK [*Seeing a fight—with a roar of joy as he springs to his feet*] At last! Bus, huh! I'll bust yuh! [*He lets drive a terrific swing, his fist landing full on the fat gentleman's face. But the gentleman stands unmoved as if nothing had happened.*]

GENTLEMAN I beg your pardon. [*Then irritably*] You have made me lose my bus. [*He claps his hands and begins to scream.*] Officer! Officer! [*Many police whistles shrill out on the instant and a whole platoon of policemen rush in on* YANK *from all sides. He tries to fight but is clubbed to the pavement and fallen upon. The crowd at the window have not moved or noticed this disturbance. The clanging gong of the patrol wagon approaches with a clamoring din.*]

[*The curtain falls.*]

## SCENE SIX

SCENE *Night of the following day. A row of cells in the prison on Blackwell's Island. The cells extend back diagonally from right front to left rear. They do not stop, but disappear in the dark background as if they ran on, numberless, into infinity. One electric bulb from the low ceiling of the narrow corridor sheds its light through the heavy steel bars of the cell at the extreme front and reveals part of the interior.* YANK *can be seen within, crouched on the edge of his cot in the attitude of Rodin's "The Thinker." His face is spotted with black and blue bruises. A bloodstained bandage is wrapped around his head.*

YANK [*Suddenly starting as if awakening from a dream, reaches out and shakes the bars—aloud to himself, wonderingly*] Steel. Dis is de Zoo, huh? [*A burst of hard barking laughter comes from the unseen occupants of the cells, runs back down the tier, and abruptly ceases.*]

VOICES [*Mockingly*] The Zoo? That's a new

name for this coop—a damn good name!
Steel, eh? You said a mouthful. This is
the old iron house.
Who is that boob talkin'?
He's the bloke they brung in out of his
head. The bulls had beat him up
fierce.

YANK [*Dully*] I musta been dreamin'. I tought
I was in a cage at de Zoo—but de apes don't talk, do
dey?

VOICES [*With mocking laughter*] You're in a
cage aw right.
A coop!
A pen!
A sty!
A kennel! [*Hard laughter—a pause*]
Say, guy! Who are you? No, never
mind lying. What are you?
Yes, tell us your sad story. What's
your game?
What did they jug yuh for?

YANK [*Dully*] I was a fireman—stokin' on de
liners. [*Then with sudden rage, rattling his cell
bars*] I'm a hairy ape, get me? And I'll bust youse
all in de jaw if yuh don't lay off kiddin' me.

VOICES Huh! You're a hard-boiled duck,
ain't you!
When you spit, it bounces! [*Laughter*]
Aw, can it. He's a regular guy. Ain't you?
What did he say he was—a ape?

YANK [*Defiantly*] Sure ting! Ain't dat what

youse all are—apes? [*A silence. Then a furious rattling of bars from down the corridor*]

A VOICE [*Thick with rage*] I'll show yuh who's a ape, yuh bum!

VOICES  Ssshh! Nix!
           Can de noise!
           Piano!
           You'll have the guard down on us!

YANK [*Scornfully*] De guard? Yuh mean de keeper, don't yuh? [*Angry exclamations from all the cells*]

VOICE [*Placatingly*] Aw, don't pay no attention to him. He's off his nut from the beatin'-up he got. Say, you guy! We're waitin' to hear what they landed you for—or ain't yuh tellin'?

YANK Sure, I'll tell youse. Sure! Why de hell not? On'y—youse won't get me. Nobody gets me but me, see? I started to tell de Judge and all he says was: "Toity days to tink it over." Tink it over! Christ, dat's all I been doin' for weeks! [*After a pause*] I was tryin' to git even with someone, see?—someone dat done me doit.

VOICES [*Cynically*]  De old stuff, I bet. Your
           goil, huh?
           Give yuh the double-cross, huh?
           That's them every time!
           Did yuh beat up de odder guy?

YANK [*Disgustedly*] Aw, yuh're all wrong! Sure dere was a skoit in it—but not what youse mean, not dat old tripe. Dis was a new kind of skoit. She was dolled up all in white—in de stokehole. I tought she was a ghost. Sure. [*A pause*]

VOICES  [*Whispering*]  Gee, he's still nutty.
Let him rave. It's fun listenin'.

YANK [*Unheeding—groping in his thoughts*] Her hands—dey was skinny and white like dey wasn't real but painted on somep'n. Dere was a million miles from me to her—twenty-five knots an hour. She was like some dead ting de cat brung in. Sure, dat's what. She didn't belong. She belonged in de window of a toy store, or on de top of a garbage can, see! Sure! [*He breaks out angrily.*] But would yuh believe it, she had de noive to do me doit. She lamped me like she was seein' somep'n broke loose from de menagerie. Christ, yuh'd oughter seen her eyes! [*He rattles the bars of his cell furiously.*] But I'll get back at her yet, you watch! And if I can't find her I'll take it out on de gang she runs wit. I'm wise to where dey hangs out now. I'll show her who belongs! I'll show her who's in de move and who ain't. You watch my smoke!

VOICES  [*Serious and joking*]  Dat's de talkin'!
Take her for all she's got!
What was this dame, anyway? Who was she, eh?

YANK  I dunno. First cabin stiff. Her old man's a millionaire, dey says—name of Douglas.

VOICES  Douglas? That's the president of the
Steel Trust, I bet.
Sure. I seen his mug in de papers.
He's filthy with dough.

VOICE  Hey, feller, take a tip from me. If you want to get back at that dame, you better join the Wobblies. You'll get some action, then.

YANK  Wobblies? What de hell's dat?

VOICE  Ain't you ever heard of the I. W. W.?

YANK  Naw. What is it?

VOICE  A gang of blokes—a tough gang. I been readin' about 'em today in the paper. The guard give me the *Sunday Times.* There's a long spiel about 'em. It's from a speech made in the Senate by a guy named Senator Queen. [*He is in the cell next to* YANK'S. *There is a rustling of paper.*] Wait'll I see if I got light enough and I'll read you. Listen. [*He reads.*] "There is a menace existing in this country today which threatens the vitals of our fair Republic —as foul a menace against the very life-blood of the American Eagle as was the foul conspiracy of Cataline against the eagles of ancient Rome!"

VOICE  [*Disgustedly*]  Aw, hell! Tell him to salt de tail of dat eagle!

VOICE  [*Reading*]  "I refer to that devil's brew of rascals, jailbirds, murderers and cutthroats who libel all honest working men by calling themselves the Industrial Workers of the World; but in the light of their nefarious plots, I call them the Industrious Wreckers of the World!"

YANK  [*With vengeful satisfaction*]  Wreckers, dat's de right dope! Dat belongs! Me for dem!

VOICE  Ssshh! [*Reading*]  "This fiendish organization is a foul ulcer on the fair body of our Democracy——"

VOICE  Democracy, hell! Give him the boid, fellers—the raspberry! [*They do.*]

VOICE  Ssshh! [*Reading*]  "Like Cato I say to this Senate, the I. W. W. must be destroyed! For they represent an ever-present dagger pointed at the heart of the greatest nation the world has ever known, where all men are born free and equal, with equal opportunities to all, where the Founding Fathers have guaranteed to each one happiness, where Truth, Honor, Liberty, Justice, and the Brotherhood of Man are a religion absorbed with one's mother's milk, taught at our father's knee, sealed, signed, and stamped upon in the glorious Constitution of these United States!" [*A perfect storm of hisses, catcalls, boos, and hard laughter*]

VOICES [*Scornfully*]  Hurrah for de Fort' of July!
Pass de hat!
Liberty!
Justice!
Honor!
Opportunity!
Brotherhood!

ALL [*With abysmal scorn*] Aw, hell!

VOICE Give that Queen Senator guy the bark! All togedder now—one—two—tree—— [*A terrific chorus of barking and yapping*]

GUARD [*From a distance*] Quiet, there, youse—or I'll get the hose. [*The noise subsides.*]

YANK [*With growling rage*] I'd like to catch dat senator guy alone for a second. I'd loin him some trute!

VOICE Ssshh! Here's where he gits down to cases on the Wobblies. [*Reads*] "They plot with fire in one hand and dynamite in the other. They stop not before murder to gain their ends, nor at the outraging of defenseless womanhood. They would tear down society, put the lowest scum in the seats of the mighty, turn Almighty God's revealed plan for the world topsy-turvy, and make of our sweet and lovely civilization a shambles, a desolation where man, God's masterpiece, would soon degenerate back to the ape!"

VOICE [*To* YANK] Hey, you guy. There's your ape stuff again.

YANK [*With a growl of fury*] I got him. So dey blow up tings, do dey? Dey turn tings round, do dey? Hey, lend me dat paper, will yuh?

VOICE Sure. Give it to him. On'y keep it to yourself, see. We don't wanter listen to no more of that slop.

VOICE Here you are. Hide it under your mattress.

YANK [*Reaching out*] Tanks. I can't read much but I kin manage. [*He sits, the paper in the hand at his side, in the attitude of Rodin's "The Thinker." A pause. Several snores from down the corridor. Suddenly* YANK *jumps to his feet with a furious groan as if some appalling thought had crashed on him—bewilderedly*] Sure--her old man —president of de Steel Trust—makes half de steel in de world—steel—where I tought I belonged— drivin' trou—movin'—in dat—to make *her*—and cage me in for her to spit on! Christ [*He shakes the bars of his cell door till the whole tier trembles. Irritated, protesting exclamations from those awakened or trying to get to sleep.*] He made dis—dis cage! Steel! *It* don't belong, dat's what! Cages, cells, locks,

bolts, bars—dat's what it means!—holdin' me down
wit him at de top! But I'll manage trou! Fire, dat
melts it! I'll be fire—under de heap—fire dat never
goes out—hot as hell—breakin' out in de night—
[*While he has been saying this last he has shaken
his cell door to a clanging accompaniment. As he
comes to the "breakin' out" he seizes one bar with
both hands and, putting his two feet up against the
others so that his position is parallel to the floor
like a monkey's, he gives a great wrench backwards.
The bar bends like a licorice stick under his tremendous strength. Just at this moment the* PRISON
GUARD *rushes in, dragging a hose behind him.*]

GUARD [*Angrily*] I'll loin youse bums to wake
me up! [*Sees* YANK] Hello, it's you, huh? Got the
D.Ts., hey? Well, I'll cure 'em. I'll drown your
snakes for yuh! [*Noticing the bar*] Hell, look at
dat bar bended! On'y a bug is strong enough for
dat!

YANK [*Glaring at him*] Or a hairy ape, yuh big
yellow bum! Look out! Here I come! [*He grabs
another bar.*]

GUARD [*Scared now—yelling off left*] Toin de
hose on, Ben!—full pressure! And call de others—
and a straitjacket! [*The curtain is falling. As it
hides* YANK *from view, there is a splattering smash
as the stream of water hits the steel of* YANK's *cell.*]

[*The curtain falls.*]

# SCENE SEVEN

SCENE *Nearly a month later. An I. W. W. local near the waterfront, showing the interior of a front room on the ground floor, and the street outside. Moonlight on the narrow street, buildings massed in black shadow. The interior of the room, which is general assembly room, office, and reading room, resembles some dingy settlement boys' club. A desk and high stool are in one corner. A table with papers, stacks of pamphlets, chairs about it, is at center. The whole is decidedly cheap, banal, commonplace and unmysterious as a room could well be. The Secretary is perched on the stool making entries in a large ledger. And eye shade casts his face into shadows. Eight or ten men, longshoremen, iron workers, and the like are grouped about the table. Two are playing checkers. One is writing a letter. Most of them are smoking pipes. A big signboard is on the wall at the rear, "Industrial Workers of the World—Local No. 57."*

YANK [*Comes down the street outside. He is dressed as in Scene Five. He moves cautiously, mysteriously. He comes to a point opposite the door; tiptoes softly up to it, listens, is impressed by the silence within, knocks carefully, as if he were guessing at the password to some secret rite. Listens. No answer. Knocks again a bit louder. No answer. Knocks impatiently, much louder.*]

SECRETARY [*Turning around on his stool*] What the hell is that—someone knocking? [*Shouts*] Come in, why don't you? [*All the men in the room look up.* YANK *opens the door slowly, gingerly, as if afraid of an ambush. He looks around for secret doors, mystery, is taken aback by the commonplaceness of the room and the men in it, thinks he may have gotten in the wrong place, then sees the signboard on the wall and is reassured.*]

YANK [*Blurts out*] Hello.

MEN [*Reservedly*] Hello.

YANK [*More easily*] I tought I'd bumped into de wrong dump.

SECRETARY [*Scrutinizing him carefully*] Maybe you have. Are you a member?

YANK Naw, not yet. Dat's what I come for—to join.

SECRETARY That's easy. What's your job—longshore?

YANK Naw. Fireman—stoker on de liners.

SECRETARY [*With satisfaction*] Welcome to our city. Glad to know you people are waking up at last. We haven't got many members in your line.

YANK Naw. Dey're all dead to de woild.

SECRETARY  Well, you can help to wake 'em. What's your name? I'll make out your card.

YANK [*Confused*]  Name? Lemme tink.

SECRETARY [*Sharply*]  Don't you know your own name?

YANK  Sure; but I been just Yank for so long—Bob, dat's it—Bob Smith.

SECRETARY [*Writing*]  Robert Smith. [*Fills out the rest of the card.*] Here you are. Cost you half a dollar.

YANK  Is dat all—four bits? Dat's easy. [*Gives the* SECRETARY *the money.*]

SECRETARY [*Throwing it in drawer*]  Thanks. Well, make yourself at home. No introductions needed. There's literature on the table. Take some of those pamphlets with you to distribute aboard ship. They may bring results. Sow the seed, only go about it right. Don't get caught and fired. We got plenty out of work. What we need is men who can hold their jobs—and work for us at the same time.

YANK  Sure. [*But he still stands, embarrassed and uneasy.*]

SECRETARY [*Looking at him—curiously*]  What did you knock for? Think we had a coon in uniform to open doors?

YANK  Naw. I tought it was locked—and dat yuh'd wanter give me the once-over trou a peephole or somep'n to see if I was right.

SECRETARY [*Alert and suspicious but with an easy laugh*]  Think we were running a crap game?

That door is never locked. What put that in your nut?

YANK [*With a knowing grin, convinced that this is all camouflage, a part of the secrecy*] Dis burg is full of bulls, ain't it?

SECRETARY [*Sharply*] What have the cops got to do with us? We're breaking no laws.

YANK [*With a knowing wink*] Sure. Youse wouldn't for woilds. Sure. I'm wise to dat.

SECRETARY You seem to be wise to a lot of stuff none of us knows about.

YANK [*With another wink*] Aw, dat's aw right, see. [*Then made a bit resentful by the suspicious glances from all sides*] Aw, can it! Youse needn't put me trou de toid degree. Can't youse see I belong? Sure! I'm reg'lar. I'll stick, get me? I'll shoot de woiks for youse. Dat's why I wanted to join in.

SECRETARY [*Breezily, feeling him out*] That's the right spirit. Only are you sure you understand what you've joined? It's all plain and aboveboard; still, some guys get a wrong slant on us. [*Sharply*] What's your notion of the purpose of the I. W. W.?

YANK Aw, I know all about it.

SECRETARY [*Sarcastically*] Well, give us some of your valuable information.

YANK [*Cunningly*] I know enough not to speak outa my toin. [*Then resentfully again*] Aw, say! I'm reg'lar. I'm wise to de game. I know yuh got to watch your step wit a stranger. For all youse know, I might be a plain-clothes dick, or somep'n, dat's what yuh're tinkin', huh? Aw, forget it! I belong, see? Ask any guy down to de docks if I don't.

## THE HAIRY APE 223

Secretary  Who said you didn't?

Yank  After I'm 'nitiated, I'll show yuh.

Secretary  [*Astounded*]  Initiated? There's no initiation.

Yank  [*Disappointed*]  Ain't there no password —no grip nor nothin'?

Secretary  What'd you think this is—the Elks —or the Black Hand?

Yank  De Elks, hell! De Black Hand, dey're a lot of yellow backstickin' Ginees. Naw. Dis is a man's gang, ain't it?

Secretary  You said it! That's why we stand on our two feet in the open. We got no secrets.

Yank  [*Surprised but admiringly*]  Yuh mean to say yuh always run wide open—like dis?

Secretary  Exactly.

Yank  Den yuh sure got your noive wit youse!

Secretary  [*Sharply*]  Just what was it made you want to join us? Come out with that straight.

Yank  Yuh call me? Well, I got noive, too! Here's my hand. Yuh wanter blow tings up, don't yuh? Well, dat's me! I belong!

Secretary  [*With pretended carelessness*]  You mean change the unequal conditions of society by legitimate direct action—or with dynamite?

Yank  Dynamite! Blow it offen de oith—steel—all de cages—all de factories, steamers, buildings, jails —de Steel Trust and all dat makes it go.

Secretary  So—that's your idea, eh? And did you have any special job in that line you wanted to propose to us? [*He makes a sign to the men, who get up cautiously one by one and group behind* YANK.]

YANK [*Boldly*] Sure, I'll come out wit it. I'll show youse I'm one of de gang. Dere's dat millionaire guy, Douglas——

SECRETARY President of the Steel Trust, you mean? Do you want to assassinate him?

YANK Naw, dat don't get yuh nothin'. I mean blow up de factory, de woiks, where he makes de steel. Dat's what I'm after—to blow up de steel, knock all de steel in de woild up to de moon. Dat'll fix tings! [*Exactly, with a touch of bravado*] I'll do it by me lonesome! I'll show yuh! Tell me where his woiks is, how to git there, all de dope. Gimme de stuff, de old butter—and watch me do de rest! Watch de smoke and see it move! I don't give a damn if dey nab me—long as it's done! I'll soive life for it —and give 'em de laugh! [*Half to himself*] And I'll write her a letter and tell her de hairy ape done it. Dat'll square tings.

SECRETARY [*Stepping away from* YANK] Very interesting. [*He gives a signal. The men, huskies all, throw themselves on* YANK *and before he knows it they have his legs and arms pinioned. But he is too flabbergasted to make a struggle, anyway. They feel him over for weapons.*]

MAN No gat, no knife. Shall we give him what's what and put the boots to him?

SECRETARY No. He isn't worth the trouble we'd get into. He's too stupid. [*He comes closer and laughs mockingly in* YANK'S *face.*] Ho-ho! By God, this is the biggest joke they've put up on us yet. Hey, you Joke! Who sent you—Burns or Pinkerton? No, by God, you're such a bonehead I'll bet you're in the Secret Service! Well, you dirty spy, you rotten agent provocator, you can go back and tell whatever skunk is paying you blood-money for betraying your brothers that he's wasting his coin. You couldn't catch a cold. And tell him that all he'll ever get on us, or ever has got, is just his own sneaking plots that he's framed up to put us in jail. We are what our manifesto says we are, neither more nor less— and we'll give him a copy of that any time he calls. And as for you—— [*He glares scornfully at* YANK, *who is sunk in an oblivious stupor.*] Oh, hell, what's the use of talking? You're a brainless ape.

YANK [*Aroused by the word to fierce but futile struggles*] What's dat, yuh Sheeny bum, yuh!

SECRETARY Throw him out, boys. [*In spite of his struggles, this is done with gusto and éclat. Propelled by several parting kicks,* YANK *lands sprawling in the middle of the narrow cobbled street. With a growl he starts to get up and storm the closed door, but stops bewildered by the confusion in his brain, pathetically impotent. He sits there, brooding, in as near to the attitude of Rodin's "Thinker" as he can get in his position.*]

YANK [*Bitterly*] So dem boids don't tink I belong, neider. Aw, to hell wit 'em! Dey're in de wrong pew—de same old bull—soapboxes and Salvation Army—no guts! Cut out an hour offen de job a day and make me happy! Gimme a dollar more a day and make me happy! Tree square a day, and cauliflowers in de front yard—ekal rights—a woman and kids—a lousy vote—and I'm all fixed for Jesus, huh? Aw, hell! What does dat get yuh? Dis ting's in your inside, but it ain't your belly. Feedin' your face—sinkers and coffee—dat don't touch it. It's way down—at de bottom. Yuh can't grab it, and yuh can't stop it. It moves, and everything moves. It stops and de whole woild stops. Dat's me now—I don't tick, see?—I'm a busted Ingersoll, dat's what. Steel was me, and I owned de woild. Now I ain't steel, and de woild owns me. Aw, hell! I can't see—it's all dark, get me? It's all wrong! [*He turns a bitter mocking face up like an ape gibbering at the moon.*] Say, youse up dere, Man in de Moon, yuh look so wise, gimme de answer, huh? Slip me de inside dope, de information right from de stable—where do I get off at, huh?

A POLICEMAN [*Who has come up the street in time to hear this last—with grim humor*] You'll get off at the station, you boob, if you don't get up out of that and keep movin'.

YANK [*Looking up at him—with a hard, bitter laugh*] Sure! Lock me up! Put me in a cage! Dat's de on'y answer yuh know. G'wan, lock me up!

POLICEMAN  What you been doin'?

YANK  Enuf to gimme life for! I was born, see? Sure, dat's de charge. Write it in de blotter. I was born, get me!

POLICEMAN [*Jocosely*] God pity your old woman! [*Then matter-of-fact*] But I've no time for kidding. You're soused. I'd run you in but it's too long a walk to the station. Come on now, get up, or I'll fan your ears with this club. Beat it now! [*He hauls* YANK *to his feet.*]

YANK [*In a vague mocking tone*] Say, where do I go from here?

POLICEMAN [*Giving him a push—with a grin, indifferently*] Go to hell.

[*The curtain falls.*]

# SCENE EIGHT

SCENE *Twilight of the next day. The monkey house at the Zoo. One spot of clear gray light falls on the front of one cage so that the interior can be seen. The other cages are vague, shrouded in shadow from which chatterings pitched in a conversational tone can be heard. On the one cage a sign from which the word "gorilla" stands out. The gigantic animal himself is seen squatting on his haunches on a bench in much the same attitude as Rodin's "Thinker."* YANK *enters from the left. Immediately a chorus of angry chattering and screeching breaks out. The gorilla turns his eyes but makes no sound or move.*

YANK [*With a hard, bitter laugh*] Welcome to your city, huh? Hail, hail, de gang's all here! [*At the sound of his voice the chattering dies away into an attentive silence.* YANK *walks up to the gorilla's cage and, leaning over the railing, stares in at its occupant, who stares back at him, silent and motion-*

less. *There is a pause of dead stillness. Then* YANK *begins to talk in a friendly confidential tone, half-mockingly, but with a deep undercurrent of sympathy.*] Say, yuh're some hard-lookin' guy, ain't yuh? I seen lots of tough nuts dat de gang called gorillas, but yuh're de foist real one I ever seen. Some chest yuh got, and shoulders, and dem arms and mits! I bet yuh got a punch in eider fist dat'd knock 'em all silly. [*This with genuine admiration. The gorilla, as if he understood, stands upright, swelling out his chest and pounding on it with his fist.* YANK *grins sympathetically.*] Sure, I get yuh. Yuh challenge de whole woild, huh? Yuh got what I was sayin' even if yuh muffed de woids. [*Then bitterness creeping in*] And why wouldn't yuh get me? Ain't we both members of de same club—de Hairy Apes? [*They stare at each other—a pause—then* YANK *goes on slowly and bitterly*] So yuh're what she seen when she looked at me, de white-faced tart! I was you to her, get me? On'y outa de cage—broke out—free to moider her, see? Sure! Dat's what she tought. She wasn't wise dat I was in a cage, too—worser'n yours—sure—a damn sight—'cause you got some chanct to bust loose—but me—— [*He grows confused.*] Aw, hell! It's all wrong, ain't it? [*A pause*] I s'pose yuh wanter know what I'm doin' here, huh? I been warmin' a bench down to de Battery—ever since last night. Sure. I seen de sun come up. Dat was pretty, too—all red and pink and green. I was looking' at de skyscrapers—steel—and all de ships comin' in, sailin' out, all over de oith—and dey was steel, too. De sun was warm, dey wasn't no clouds, and dere was a

*Paddy's imagery*

breeze blowin'. Sure, it was great stuff. I got it aw right—what Paddy said about dat bein' de right dope—on'y I couldn't get *in* it, see? I couldn't belong in dat. It was over my head. And I kept tinkin'— and den I beat it up here to see what youse was like. And I waited till dey was all gone to git yuh alone. Say, how d'yuh feel sittin' in dat pen all de time, havin' to stand for 'em comin' and starin' at yuh—de white-faced, skinny tarts and de boobs what marry 'em—makin' fun of yuh, laughin' at yuh, gittin' scared of yuh—damn 'em! [*He pounds on the rail with his fist. The gorilla rattles the bars of his cage and snarls. All the other monkeys set up an angry chattering in the darkness.* YANK *goes on excitedly*] Sure! Dat's de way it hits me, too. On'y yuh're lucky, see? Yuh don't belong wit 'em and you know it. But me, I belong wit 'em—but I don't, see? Dey don't belong wit me, dat's what. Get me? Tinkin' is hard—— [*He passes one hand across his forehead with a painful gesture. The gorilla growls impatiently.* YANK *goes on gropingly*] It's dis way, what I'm drivin' at. Youse can sit and dope dream in de past, green woods, de jungle and de rest of it. Den yuh belong and dey don't. Den yuh kin laugh at 'em, see? Yuh're de champ of de woild. But me—I ain't got no past to tink in, nor nothin' dat's comin', on'y what's now—and dat don't belong. Sure, you're de best off! Yuh can't tink, can yuh? Yuh can't talk neider. But I kin make a bluff at talkin' and tinkin' —a'most git away wit it—a'most!—and dat's where de joker comes in. [*He laughs.*] I ain't on oith and I ain't in heaven, get me? I'm in de middle tryin' to separate 'em, takin' all de woist punches from bot' of 'em. Maybe dat's what dey call hell, huh? But you, yuh're at de bottom. You belong! Sure! Yuh're de on'y one in de woild dat does, yuh lucky stiff! [*The gorilla growls proudly.*] And dat's why dey gotter put yuh in a cage, see? [*The gorilla roars angrily.*] Sure! Yuh get me. It beats it when you try to tink it or talk it—it's way down—deep—behind—you 'n' me we feel it. Sure! Bot' members of dis club! [*He laughs—then in a savage tone*] What de hell! T' hell wit it! A little action, dat's our meat! Dat belongs! Knock 'em down and keep bustin' 'em till dey croaks yuh wit a gat—wit steel! Sure! Are yuh game? Dey've looked at youse, ain't dey—in a cage? Wanter get even? Wanter wind up like a sport 'stead of croakin' slow in dere? [*The gorilla roars an emphatic affirmative.* YANK *goes on with a sort of furious exaltation*] Sure! Yuh're reg'lar! Yuh'll stick to de finish! Me 'n' you, huh?—bot' members of this club! We'll put up one last star bout dat'll knock 'em offen deir seats! Dey'll have to make de cages stronger after we're trou! [*The gorilla is straining at his bars, growling, hopping from one foot to the other.* YANK *takes a jimmy from under his coat and forces the lock on the cage door. He throws this open.*] Pardon from de governor! Step out and shake hands! I'll take yuh for a walk down Fif' Avenoo. We'll knock 'em offen de oith and croak wit de band playin'. Come on, Brother. [*The gorilla scrambles gingerly out of his cage. Goes to* YANK *and stands looking at him.* YANK *keeps his mocking tone—holds out his hand.*] Shake—de secret grip of our order.

## 232  THE HAIRY APE

[*Something, the tone of mockery, perhaps, suddenly enrages the animal. With a spring he wraps his huge arms around* YANK *in a murderous hug. There is a crackling snap of crushed ribs—a gasping cry, still mocking, from* YANK.] Hey, I didn't say kiss me! [*The gorilla lets the crushed body slip to the floor; stands over it uncertainly, considering; then picks it up, throws it in the cage, shuts the door, and shuffles off menacingly into the darkness at left. A great uproar of frightened chattering and whimpering comes from the other cages. Then* YANK *moves, groaning, opening his eyes, and there is silence. He mutters painfully.*] Say—dey oughter match him —wit Zybszko. He got me, aw right. I'm trou. Even him didn't tink I belonged. [*Then, with sudden passionate despair*] Christ, where do I get off at? Where do I fit in? [*Checking himself as suddenly*] Aw, what de hell! No squawkin', see! No quittin', get me! Croak wit your boots on! [*He grabs hold of the bars of the cage and hauls himself painfully to his feet—looks around him bewilderedly—forces a mocking laugh.*] In de cage, huh? [*In the strident tones of a circus barker*] Ladies and gents, step forward and take a slant at de one and only—[*His voice weakened*]—one and original—Hairy Ape from de wilds of—— [*He slips in a heap on the floor and dies. The monkeys set up a chattering, whimpering wail. And, perhaps, the Hairy Ape at last belongs.*]

[*The curtain falls.*]

EUGENE O'NEILL was born on October 16, 1888, in New York City. His father was James O'Neill, the famous dramatic actor; and during his early years O'Neill traveled much with his parents. In 1909 he went on a gold-prospecting expedition to South America; he later shipped as a seaman to Buenos Aires, worked at various occupations in the Argentine and tended mules on a cattle steamer to South Africa. He returned to New York destitute, then worked briefly as a reporter on a newspaper in New London, Connecticut, at which point an attack of tuberculosis sent him for six months to a sanitarium. This event marked the turning point in his career, and shortly after, at the age of twenty-four, he began his first play. His major works include *The Emperor Jones,* 1920; *The Hairy Ape,* 1921; *Desire Under the Elms,* 1924; *The Great God Brown,* 1925; *Strange Interlude,* 1926, 1927; *Mourning Becomes Electra,* 1929, 1931; *Ah, Wilderness,* 1933; *Days Without End,* 1934; *A Moon for the Misbegotten,* 1945; *The Iceman Cometh,* 1946; and several plays produced posthumously, including *Long Day's Journey into Night, A Touch of the Poet* and *Hughie.* Eugene O'Neill died in 1953.

## VINTAGE BELLES—LETTRES

| | | |
|---|---|---|
| V-418 | **AUDEN, W. H.** / The Dyer's Hand |
| V-887 | **AUDEN, W. H.** / Forewords and Afterwords |
| V-271 | **BEDIER, JOSEPH** / Tristan and Iseult |
| V-512 | **BLOCH, MARC** / The Historian's Craft |
| V-572 | **BRIDGEHAMPTON** / Bridgehampton Works & Days |
| V-161 | **BROWN, NORMAN O.** / Closing Time |
| V-544 | **BROWN, NORMAN O.** / Hermes the Thief |
| V-419 | **BROWN, NORMAN O.** / Love's Body |
| V-75 | **CAMUS, ALBERT** / The Myth of Sisyphus and Other Essays |
| V-30 | **CAMUS, ALBERT** / The Rebel |
| V-608 | **CARR, JOHN DICKSON** / The Life of Sir Arthur Conan Doyle: The Man Who Was Sherlock Holmes |
| V-407 | **HARDWICK, ELIZABETH** / Seduction and Betrayal: Women and Literature |
| V-244 | **HERRIGEL, EUGEN** / The Method of Zen |
| V-663 | **HERRIGEL, EUGEN** / Zen in the Art of Archery |
| V-201 | **HUGHES, H. STUART** / Consciousness & Society |
| V-235 | **KAPLAN, ABRAHAM** / New World of Philosophy |
| V-337 | **KAUFMANN, WALTER (trans.) AND FRIEDRICH NIETZSCHE** / Beyond Good and Evil |
| V-369 | **KAUFMANN, WALTER (trans.) AND FRIEDRICH NIETZSCHE** / The Birth of Tragedy and the Case of Wagner |
| V-985 | **KAUFMANN, WALTER (trans.) AND FRIEDRICH NIETZSCHE** / The Gay Science |
| V-401 | **KAUFMANN, WALTER (trans.) AND FRIEDRICH NIETZSCHE** / On the Genealogy of Morals and Ecce Homo |
| V-437 | **KAUFMANN, WALTER (trans.) AND FRIEDRICH NIETZSCHE** / The Will to Power |
| V-995 | **KOTT, JAN** / The Eating of the Gods: An Interpretation of Greek Tragedy |
| V-685 | **LESSING, DORIS** / A Small Personal Voice: Essays, Reviews, Interviews |
| V-329 | **LINDBERGH, ANNE MORROW** / Gift from the Sea |
| V-479 | **MALRAUX, ANDRE** / Man's Fate |
| V-406 | **MARCUS, STEVEN** / Engels, Manchester and the Working Class |
| V-58 | **MENCKEN, H. L.** / Prejudices (Selected by James T. Farrell) |
| V-25 | **MENCKEN, H. L.** / The Vintage Mencken (Gathered by Alistair Cooke) |
| V-151 | **MOFFAT, MARY JANE AND CHARLOTTE PAINTER (eds.)** / Revelations: Diaries of Women |
| V-926 | **MUSTARD, HELEN (trans.)** / Heinrich Heine: Selected Works |
| V-337 | **NIETZSCHE, FRIEDRICH AND WALTER KAUFMANN (trans.)** / Beyond Good and Evil |
| V-369 | **NIETZSCHE, FRIEDRICH AND WALTER KAUFMANN (trans.)** / The Birth of Tragedy and the Case of Wagner |
| V-985 | **NIETZSCHE, FRIEDRICH AND WALTER KAUFMANN (trans.)** / The Gay Science |
| V-401 | **NIETZSCHE, FRIEDRICH AND WALTER KAUFMANN (trans.)** / On the Genealogy of Morals and Ecce Homo |

| | |
|---|---|
| V-437 | **NIETZSCHE, FRIEDRICH AND WALTER KAUFMANN (trans.)** / The Will to Power |
| V-672 | **OUSPENSKY, P. D.** / The Fourth Way |
| V-524 | **OUSPENSKY, P. D.** / A New Model of the Universe |
| V-943 | **OUSPENSKY, P. D.** / The Psychology of Man's Possible Evolution |
| V-639 | **OUSPENSKY, P. D.** / Tertium Organum |
| V-151 | **PAINTER, CHARLOTTE AND MARY JANE MOFFAT (eds.)** / Revelations: Diaries of Women |
| V-986 | **PAUL, DAVID (trans.)** / Poison & Vision: Poems & Prose of Baudelaire, Mallarme and Rimbaud |
| V-598 | **PROUST, MARCEL** / The Captive |
| V-597 | **PROUST, MARCEL** / Cities of the Plain |
| V-596 | **PROUST, MARCEL** / The Guermantes Way |
| V-594 | **PROUST, MARCEL** / Swann's Way |
| V-599 | **PROUST, MARCEL** / The Sweet Cheat Gone |
| V-595 | **PROUST, MARCEL** / Within a Budding Grove |
| V-899 | **SAMUEL, MAURICE** / The World of Sholom Aleichem |
| V-415 | **SHATTUCK, ROGER** / The Banquet Years (revised) |
| V-278 | **STEVENS, WALLACE** / The Necessary Angel |
| V-761 | **WATTS, ALAN** / Behold the Spirit |
| V-923 | **WATTS, ALAN** / Beyond Theology: The Art of Godmanship |
| V-853 | **WATTS, ALAN** / The Book: the Taboo Against Knowing Who You Are |
| V-999 | **WATTS, ALAN** / Cloud-Hidden, Whereabouts Unknown: A Mountain Journal |
| V-665 | **WATTS, ALAN** / Does it Matter? |
| V-951 | **WATTS, ALAN** / In My Own Way |
| V-299 | **WATTS, ALAN** / The Joyous Cosmology |
| V-592 | **WATTS, ALAN** / Nature, Man and Woman |
| V-609 | **WATTS, ALAN** / Psychotherapy East & West |
| V-835 | **WATTS, ALAN** / The Supreme Identity |
| V-298 | **WATTS, ALAN** / The Way of Zen |
| V-870 | **WIESEL, ELIE** / Souls on Fire |

## VINTAGE FICTION, POETRY, AND PLAYS

- V-814 **ABE, KOBO** / The Woman in the Dunes
- V-2014 **AUDEN, W. H.** / Collected Longer Poems
- V-2015 **AUDEN, W. H.** / Collected Shorter Poems 1927-1957
- V-102 **AUDEN, W. H.** / Selected Poetry of W. H. Auden
- V-601 **AUDEN, W. H. AND PAUL B. TAYLOR (trans.)** / The Elder Edda
- V-20 **BABIN, MARIA-THERESA AND STAN STEINER (eds.)** / Borinquen: An Anthology of Puerto-Rican Literature
- V-271 **BEDIER, JOSEPH** / Tristan and Iseult
- V-523 **BELLAMY, JOE DAVID (ed.)** / Superfiction or The American Story Transformed: An Anthology
- V-72 **BERNIKOW, LOUISE (ed.)** / The World Split Open: Four Centuries of Women Poets in England and America 1552-1950
- V-321 **BOLT, ROBERT** / A Man for All Seasons
- V-21 **BOWEN, ELIZABETH** / The Death of the Heart
- V-294 **BRADBURY, RAY** / The Vintage Bradbury
- V-670 **BRECHT, BERTOLT (ed. by Ralph Manheim and John Willett)** / Collected Plays, Vol. 1
- V-759 **BRECHT, BERTOLT (ed. by Ralph Manheim and John Willett)** / Collected Plays, Vol. 5
- V-216 **BRECHT, BERTOLT (ed. by Ralph Manheim and John Willett)** / Collected Plays, Vol. 7
- V-819 **BRECHT, BERTOLT (ed. by Ralph Manheim and John Willett)** / Collected Plays, Vol. 9
- V-841 **BYNNER, WITTER AND KIANG KANG-HU (eds.)** / The Jade Mountain: A Chinese Anthology
- V-207 **CAMUS, ALBERT** / Caligula & Three Other Plays
- V-281 **CAMUS, ALBERT** / Exile and the Kingdom
- V-223 **CAMUS, ALBERT** / The Fall
- V-865 **CAMUS, ALBERT** / A Happy Death: A Novel
- V-626 **CAMUS, ALBERT** / Lyrical and Critical Essays
- V-75 **CAMUS, ALBERT** / The Myth of Sisyphus and Other Essays
- V-258 **CAMUS, ALBERT** / The Plague
- V-245 **CAMUS, ALBERT** / The Possessed
- V-30 **CAMUS, ALBERT** / The Rebel
- V-2 **CAMUS, ALBERT** / The Stranger
- V-28 **CATHER, WILLA** / Five Stories
- V-705 **CATHER, WILLA** / A Lost Lady
- V-200 **CATHER, WILLA** / My Mortal Enemy
- V-179 **CATHER, WILLA** / Obscure Destinies
- V-252 **CATHER, WILLA** / One of Ours
- V-913 **CATHER, WILLA** / The Professor's House
- V-434 **CATHER, WILLA** / Sapphira and the Slave Girl
- V-680 **CATHER, WILLA** / Shadows on the Rock
- V-684 **CATHER, WILLA** / Youth and the Bright Medusa
- V-140 **CERF, BENNETT (ed.)** / Famous Ghost Stories
- V-203 **CERF, BENNETT (ed.)** / Four Contemporary American Plays
- V-127 **CERF, BENNETT (ed.)** / Great Modern Short Stories
- V-326 **CERF, CHRISTOPHER (ed.)** / The Vintage Anthology of Science Fantasy

| | |
|---|---|
| V-293 | **CHAUCER, GEOFFREY** / The Canterbury Tales (a prose version in Modern English) |
| V-142 | **CHAUCER, GEOFFREY** / Troilus and Cressida |
| V-723 | **CHERNYSHEVSKY, N. G.** / What Is to Be Done? |
| V-173 | **CONFUCIUS (trans. by Arthur Waley)** / Analects |
| V-155 | **CONRAD, JOSEPH** / Three Great Tales: The Nigger of the Narcissus, Heart of Darkness, Youth |
| V-10 | **CRANE, STEPHEN** / Stories and Tales |
| V-126 | **DANTE, ALIGHIERI** / The Divine Comedy |
| V-177 | **DINESEN, ISAK** / Anecdotes of Destiny |
| V-431 | **DINESEN, ISAK** / Ehrengard |
| V-752 | **DINESEN, ISAK** / Last Tales |
| V-740 | **DINESEN, ISAK** / Out of Africa |
| V-807 | **DINESEN, ISAK** / Seven Gothic Tales |
| V-62 | **DINESEN, ISAK** / Shadows on the Grass |
| V-205 | **DINESEN, ISAK** / Winter's Tales |
| V-721 | **DOSTOYEVSKY, FYODOR** / Crime and Punishment |
| V-722 | **DOSTOYEVSKY, FYODOR** / The Brothers Karamazov |
| V-780 | **FAULKNER, WILLIAM** / Absalom, Absalom! |
| V-254 | **FAULKNER, WILLIAM** / As I Lay Dying |
| V-884 | **FAULKNER, WILLIAM** / Go Down, Moses |
| V-139 | **FAULKNER, WILLIAM** / The Hamlet |
| V-792 | **FAULKNER, WILLIAM** / Intruder in the Dust |
| V-189 | **FAULKNER, WILLIAM** / Light in August |
| V-282 | **FAULKNER, WILLIAM** / The Mansion |
| V-339 | **FAULKNER, WILLIAM** / The Reivers |
| V-412 | **FAULKNER, WILLIAM** / Requiem For A Nun |
| V-381 | **FAULKNER, WILLIAM** / Sanctuary |
| V-5 | **FAULKNER, WILLIAM** / The Sound and the Fury |
| V-184 | **FAULKNER, WILLIAM** / The Town |
| V-351 | **FAULKNER, WILLIAM** / The Unvanquished |
| V-262 | **FAULKNER, WILLIAM** / The Wild Palms |
| V-149 | **FAULKNER, WILLIAM** / Three Famous Short Novels: Spotted Horses, Old Man, The Bear |
| V-45 | **FORD, FORD MADOX** / The Good Soldier |
| V-7 | **FORSTER, E. M.** Howards End |
| V-40 | **FORSTER, E. M.** / The Longest Journey |
| V-187 | **FORSTER, E. M.** / A Room With a View |
| V-61 | **FORSTER, E. M.** / Where Angels Fear to Tread |
| V-219 | **FRISCH, MAX** / I'm Not Stiller |
| V-842 | **GIDE, ANDRE** / The Counterfeiters |
| V-8 | **GIDE, ANDRE** / The Immoralist |
| V-96 | **GIDE, ANDRE** / Lafcadio's Adventures |
| V-27 | **GIDE, ANDRE** / Strait Is the Gate |
| V-66 | **GIDE, ANDRE** / Two Legends: Oedipus and Theseus |
| V-958 | **von GOETHE, JOHANN WOLFGANG (ELIZABETH MAYER, LOUISE BOGAN & W. H. AUDEN, trans.)** / The Sorrows of Young Werther and Novella |
| V-300 | **GRASS, GUNTER** / The Tin Drum |
| V-425 | **GRAVES, ROBERT** / Claudius the God |
| V-182 | **GRAVES, ROBERT** / I, Claudius |
| V-717 | **GUERNEY, B. G. (ed.)** / An Anthology of Russian Literature in the Soviet Period: From Gorki to Pasternak |

| | | |
|---|---|---|
| V-829 | **HAMMETT, DASHIELL** / | The Big Knockover |
| V-2013 | **HAMMETT, DASHIELL** / | The Continental Op |
| V-827 | **HAMMETT, DASHIELL** / | The Dain Curse |
| V-773 | **HAMMETT, DASHIELL** / | The Glass Key |
| V-772 | **HAMMETT, DASHIELL** / | The Maltese Falcon |
| V-828 | **HAMMETT, DASHIELL** / | The Red Harvest |
| V-774 | **HAMMETT, DASHIELL** / | The Thin Man |
| V-781 | **HAMSUN, KNUT** / | Growth of the Soil |
| V-896 | **HATCH, JAMES AND VICTORIA SULLIVAN (eds.)** / Plays by and About Women |
| V-15 | **HAWTHORNE, NATHANIEL** / | Short Stories |
| V-610 | **HSU, KAI-YU** / The Chinese Literary Scene: A Writer's Visit to the People's Republic |
| V-910 | **HUGHES, LANGSTON** / | Selected Poems of Langston Hughes |
| V-304 | **HUGHES, LANGSTON** / | The Ways of White Folks |
| V-158 | **ISHERWOOD, CHRISTOPHER AND W. H. AUDEN** / Two Plays: The Dog Beneath the Skin and The Ascent of F6 |
| V-295 | **JEFFERS, ROBINSON** / | Selected Poems |
| V-380 | **JOYCE, JAMES** / | Ulysses |
| V-991 | **KAFKA, FRANZ** / | The Castle |
| V-484 | **KAFKA, FRANZ** / | The Trial |
| V-841 | **KANG-HU, KIANG AND WITTER BYNNER** / The Jade Mountain: A Chinese Anthology |
| V-508 | **KOCH, KENNETH** / | The Art of Love |
| V-915 | **KOCH, KENNETH** / | A Change of Hearts |
| V-467 | **KOCH, KENNETH** / | The Red Robbins |
| V-82 | **KOCH, KENNETH** / | Wishes, Lies and Dreams |
| V-134 | **LAGERKVIST, PAR** / | Barabbas |
| V-240 | **LAGERKVIST, PAR** / | The Sibyl |
| V-776 | **LAING, R. D.** / | Knots |
| V-23 | **LAWRENCE, D. H.** / | The Plumed Serpent |
| V-71 | **LAWRENCE, D. H.** / | St. Mawr & The Man Who Died |
| V-329 | **LINDBERGH, ANNE MORROW** / | Gift from the Sea |
| V-822 | **LINDBERGH, ANNE MORROW** / | The Unicorn and Other Poems |
| V-479 | **MALRAUX, ANDRE** / | Man's Fate |
| V-180 | **MANN, THOMAS** / | Buddenbrooks |
| V-3 | **MANN, THOMAS** / | Death in Venice and Seven Other Stories |
| V-297 | **MANN, THOMAS** / | Doctor Faustus |
| V-497 | **MANN, THOMAS** / | The Magic Mountain |
| V-86 | **MANN, THOMAS** / | The Transposed Heads |
| V-36 | **MANSFIELD, KATHERINE** / | Stories |
| V-137 | **MAUGHAM, W. SOMERSET** / | Of Human Bondage |
| V-720 | **MIRSKY, D. S.** / A History of Russian Literature: From Its Beginnings to 1900 |
| V-883 | **MISHIMA, YUKIO** / | Five Modern Nō Plays |
| V-151 | **MOFFAT, MARY JANE AND CHARLOTTE PAINTER** / Revelations: Diaries of Women |
| V-851 | **MORGAN, ROBIN** / | Monster |
| V-926 | **MUSTARD, HELEN (trans.)** / | Heinrich Heine: Selected Works |
| V-901 | **NEMIROFF, ROBERT (ed.)** / Les Blancs: The Collected Last Plays of Lorraine Hansberry |
| V-925 | **NGUYEN, DU** / | The Tale of Kieu |

| V-125 | OATES, WHITNEY J. AND EUGENE O'NEILL, Jr. (eds.) / Seven Famous Greek Plays |
|---|---|
| V-973 | O'HARA, FRANK / Selected Poems of Frank O'Hara |
| V-855 | O'NEILL, EUGENE / Anna Christie, The Emperor Jones, The Hairy Ape |
| V-18 | O'NEILL, EUGENE / The Iceman Cometh |
| V-236 | O'NEILL, EUGENE / A Moon For the Misbegotten |
| V-856 | O'NEILL, EUGENE / Seven Plays of the Sea |
| V-276 | O'NEILL, EUGENE / Six Short Plays |
| V-165 | O'NEILL, EUGENE / Three Plays: Desire Under the Elms, Strange Interlude, Mourning Becomes Electra |
| V-125 | O'NEILL, EUGENE, JR. AND WHITNEY J. OATES (eds.) / Seven Famous Greek Plays |
| V-151 | PAINTER, CHARLOTTE AND MARY JANE MOFFAT / Revelations: Diaries of Women |
| V-907 | PERELMAN, S. J. / Crazy Like a Fox |
| V-466 | PLATH, SYLVIA / The Colossus and Other Poems |
| V-232 | PRITCHETT, V. S. / Midnight Oil |
| V-598 | PROUST, MARCEL / The Captive |
| V-597 | PROUST, MARCEL / Cities of the Plain |
| V-596 | PROUST, MARCEL / The Guermantes Way |
| V-600 | PROUST, MARCEL / The Past Recaptured |
| V-594 | PROUST, MARCEL / Swann's Way |
| V-599 | PROUST, MARCEL / The Sweet Cheat Gone |
| V-595 | PROUST, MARCEL / Within A Budding Grove |
| V-714 | PUSHKIN, ALEXANDER / The Captain's Daughter and Other Stories |
| V-976 | QUASHA, GEORGE AND JEROME ROTHENBERG (eds.) / America a Prophecy: A Reading of American Poetry from Pre-Columbian Times to the Present |
| V-80 | REDDY, T. J. / Less Than a Score, But A Point: Poems by T. J. Reddy |
| V-504 | RENAULT, MARY / The Bull From the Sea |
| V-653 | RENAULT, MARY / The Last of the Wine |
| V-24 | RHYS, JEAN / After Leaving Mr. Mackenzie |
| V-42 | RHYS, JEAN / Good Morning Midnight |
| V-319 | RHYS, JEAN / Quartet |
| V-2016 | ROSEN, KENNETH (ed.) / The Man to Send Rain Clouds: Contemporary Stories by American Indians |
| V-976 | ROTHENBERG, JEROME AND GEORGE QUASHA (eds.) / America a Prophecy: A New Reading of American Poetry From Pre-Columbian Times to the Present |
| V-41 | SARGENT, PAMELA (ed.) / Women of Wonder: Science Fiction Stories by Women About Women |
| V-838 | SARTRE, JEAN-PAUL / The Age of Reason |
| V-238 | SARTRE, JEAN-PAUL / The Condemned of Altona |
| V-65 | SARTRE, JEAN-PAUL / The Devil & The Good Lord & Two Other Plays |
| V-16 | SARTRE, JEAN-PAUL / No Exit and Three Other Plays |
| V-839 | SARTRE, JEAN-PAUL / The Reprieve |
| V-74 | SARTRE, JEAN-PAUL / The Trojan Women: Euripides |
| V-840 | SARTRE, JEAN-PAUL / Troubled Sleep |

| | |
|---|---|
| V-607 | **SCORTIA, THOMAS N. AND GEORGE ZEBROWSKI (eds.)** / Human-Machines: An Anthology of Stories About Cyborgs |
| V-330 | **SHOLOKHOV, MIKHAIL** / And Quiet Flows the Don |
| V-331 | **SHOLOKHOV, MIKHAIL** / The Don Flows Home to the Sea |
| V-447 | **SILVERBERG, ROBERT** / Born With the Dead: Three Novellas About the Spirit of Man |
| V-945 | **SNOW, LOIS WHEELER** / China On Stage |
| V-133 | **STEIN, GERTRUDE** / Autobiography of Alice B. Toklas |
| V-826 | **STEIN, GERTRUDE** / Everybody's Autobiography |
| V-941 | **STEIN, GERTRUDE** / The Geographical History of America |
| V-797 | **STEIN, GERTRUDE** / Ida |
| V-695 | **STEIN, GERTRUDE** / Last Operas and Plays |
| V-477 | **STEIN, GERTRUDE** / Lectures in America |
| V-153 | **STEIN, GERTRUDE** / Three Lives |
| V-710 | **STEIN, GERTRUDE & CARL VAN VECHTEN (ed.)** / Selected Writings of Gertrude Stein |
| V-20 | **STEINER, STAN AND MARIA-THERESA BABIN (eds.)** / Borinquen: An Anthology of Puerto-Rican Literature |
| V-770 | **STEINER, STAN AND LUIS VALDEZ (eds.)** / Aztlan: An Anthology of Mexican-American Literature |
| V-769 | **STEINER, STAN AND SHIRLEY HILL WITT (eds.)** / The Way: An Anthology of American Indian Literature |
| V-768 | **STEVENS, HOLLY (ed.)** / The Palm at the End of the Mind: Selected Poems & A Play by Wallace Stevens |
| V-278 | **STEVENS, WALLACE** / The Necessary Angel |
| V-896 | **SULLIVAN, VICTORIA AND JAMES HATCH (eds.)** / Plays By and About Women |
| V-63 | **SVEVO, ITALO** / Confessions of Zeno |
| V-178 | **SYNGE, J. M.** / Complete Plays |
| V-601 | **TAYLOR, PAUL B. AND W. H. AUDEN (trans.)** / The Elder Edda |
| V-443 | **TROUPE, QUINCY AND RAINER SCHULTE (eds.)** / Giant Talk: An Anthology of Third World Writings |
| V-770 | **VALDEZ, LUIS AND STAN STEINER (eds.)** / Aztlan: An Anthology of Mexican-American Literature |
| V-710 | **VAN VECHTEN, CARL (ed.) AND GERTRUDE STEIN** / Selected Writings of Gertrude Stein |
| V-870 | **WIESEL, ELIE** / Souls on Fire |
| V-769 | **WITT, SHIRLEY HILL AND STAN STEINER (eds.)** / The Way: An Anthology of American Indian Literature |
| V-2028 | **WODEHOUSE, P. G.** / The Code of the Woosters |
| V-2026 | **WODEHOUSE, P. G.** / Leave It to Psmith |
| V-2027 | **WODEHOUSE, P. G.** / Mulliner Nights |
| V-607 | **ZEBROWSKI, GEORGE AND THOMAS N. SCORTIA (eds.)** / Human-Machines: An Anthology of Stories About Cyborgs |

## VINTAGE POLITICAL SCIENCE AND SOCIAL CRITICISM

| | |
|---|---|
| V-568 | ALINSKY, SAUL D. / Reveille for Radicals |
| V-736 | ALINSKY, SAUL D. / Rules for Radicals |
| V-726 | ALLENDE, PRESIDENT SALVADOR AND REGIS DEBRAY / The Chilian Revolution |
| V-286 | ARIES, PHILIPPE / Centuries of Childhood |
| V-604 | BAILYN, BERNARD / Origins of American Politics |
| V-334 | BALTZELL, E. DIGBY / The Protestant Establishment |
| V-571 | BARTH, ALAN / Prophets With Honor: Great Dissents & Great Dissenters in the Supreme Court |
| V-791 | BAXANDALL, LEE (ed.) AND WILHELM REICH / Sex-Pol.: Essays 1929-1934 |
| V-60 | BECKER, CARL L. / The Declaration of Independence |
| V-563 | BEER, SAMUEL H. / British Politics in the Collectivist Age |
| V-994 | BERGER, PETER & BRIGITTE AND HANSFRIED KELLNER / The Homeless Mind: Modernization and Consciousness |
| V-77 | BINZEN, PETER / Whitetown, USA |
| V-513 | BOORSTIN, DANIEL J. / The Americans: The Colonial Experience |
| V-11 | BOORSTIN, DANIEL J. / The Americans: The Democratic Experience |
| V-358 | BOORSTIN, DANIEL J. / The Americans: The National Experience |
| V-501 | BOORSTIN, DANIEL J. / Democracy and Its Discontents: Reflections on Everyday America |
| V-414 | BOTTOMORE, T. B. / Classics in Modern Society |
| V-742 | BOTTOMORE, T. B. / Sociology: A Guide to Problems & Literature |
| V-305 | BREINES, SIMON AND WILLIAM J. DEAN / The Pedestrian Revolution: Streets Without Cars |
| V-44 | BRINTON, CRANE / The Anatomy of Revolution |
| V-30 | CAMUS, ALBERT / The Rebel |
| V-966 | CAMUS, ALBERT / Resistance, Rebellion & Death |
| V-33 | CARMICHAEL, STOKELY AND CHARLES HAMILTON / Black Power |
| V-2024 | CARO, ROBERT A. / The Power Broker: Robert Moses and The Fall of New York |
| V-862 | CASE, JOHN AND GERRY HUNNIUS AND DAVID G. GARSON / Workers Control: A Reader on Labor and Social Change |
| V-98 | CASH, W. J. / The Mind of the South |
| V-555 | CHOMSKY, NOAM / American Power and the New Mandarins |
| V-248 | CHOMSKY, NOAM / Peace in the Middle East? Reflections of Justice and Nationhood |
| V-815 | CHOMSKY, NOAM / Problems of Knowledge and Freedom |
| V-788 | CIRINO, ROBERT / Don't Blame the People |
| V-17 | CLARKE, TED AND DENIS JAFFE (eds.) / Worlds Apart: Young People and The Drug Programs |

| | |
|---|---|
| V-383 | **CLOWARD, RICHARD AND FRANCES FOX PIVEN** / The Politics of Turmoil: Essays on Poverty, Race and The Urban Crisis |
| V-743 | **CLOWARD, RICHARD AND FRANCES FOX PIVEN** / Regulating the Poor: The Functions of Public Welfare |
| V-940 | **COBB, JONATHAN AND RICHARD SENNET** / Hidden Injuries of Class |
| V-311 | **CREMIN, LAWRENCE A.** / The Genius of American Education |
| V-519 | **CREMIN, LAWRENCE A.** / The Transformation of the School |
| V-808 | **CUMMING, ROBERT D. (ed.)** / The Philosophy of Jean-Paul Sartre |
| V-2019 | **CUOMO, MARIO** / Forest Hills Diary: The Crisis of Low-Income Housing |
| V-305 | **DEAN, WILLIAM J. AND SIMON BREINES** / The Pedestrian Revolution: Streets Without Cars |
| V-726 | **DEBRAY, REGIS AND PRESIDENT SALVADOR ALLENDE** / The Chilean Revolution |
| V-638 | **DENNISON, GEORGE** / The Lives of Children |
| V-746 | **DEUTSCHER, ISSAC** / The Prophet Armed |
| V-748 | **DEUTSCHER, ISSAC** / The Prophet Outcast |
| V-617 | **DEVLIN, BERNADETTE** / The Price of My Soul |
| V-671 | **DOMHOFF, G. WILLIAM** / The Higher Circles |
| V-812 | **ELLUL, JACQUES** / The Political Illusion |
| V-874 | **ELLUL, JACQUES** / Propaganda: The Formation of Men's Attitudes |
| V-390 | **ELLUL, JACQUES** / The Technological Society |
| V-143 | **EMERSON, THOMAS I.** / The System of Freedom of Expression |
| V-396 | **EPSTEIN, EDWARD JAY** / Between Fact and Fiction: The Problem of Journalism |
| V-998 | **EPSTEIN, EDWARD JAY** / News from Nowhere: Television and The News |
| V-405 | **ESHERICK, JOSEPH W. (ed.) AND JOHN S. SERVICE** / Lost Chance in China: The World War II Despatches of John S. Service |
| V-803 | **EVANS, ROWLAND JR. AND ROBERT D. NOVAK** / Nixon in the White House: The Frustration of Power |
| V-802 | **FALK, RICHARD A.** / This Endangered Planet: Prospects and Proposals for Human Survival |
| V-2002 | **FERNBACH, DAVID AND KARL MARX** / Political Writings Vol. I: The Revolutions of 1848 |
| V-2003 | **FERNBACH, DAVID AND KARL MARX** / Political Writings Vol. II: Surveys from Exile |
| V-2004 | **FERNBACH, DAVID AND KARL MARX** / Political Writings Vol. III: The First International and After |
| V-225 | **FISCHER, LOUIS (ed.)** / The Essential Gandhi |
| V-927 | **FITZGERALD, FRANCES** / Fire in the Lake: The Vietnamese and the Americans in Vietnam |

- V-316 **FREEMAN, S. DAVID** / Energy: The New Era
- V-368 **FRIENDENBERG, EDGAR Z.** / Coming of Age in America
- V-409 **FRIENDLY, FRED W.** / Due to Circumstances Beyond Our Control
- V-378 **FULBRIGHT, J. WILLIAM** / The Arrogance of Power
- V-846 **FULBRIGHT, J. WILLIAM** / The Crippled Giant
- V-491 **GANS, HERBERT J.** / The Levittowners
- V-167 **GANS, HERBERT J.** / More Equality
- V-862 **GARSON, DAVID G. AND GERRY HUNNIUS AND JOHN CASE** / Workers Control: A Reader in Labor and Social Change
- V-2018 **GAYLIN, WILLARD** / Partial Justice: A Study of Bias in Sentencing
- V-183 **GOLDMAN, ERIC F.** / The Crucial Decade—and After: America 1945-1960
- V-31 **GOLDMAN, ERIC F.** / Rendez-vous With Destiny
- V-174 **GOODMAN, PAUL AND PERCIVAL** / Communitas
- V-325 **GOODMAN, PAUL** / Compulsory Mis-education and The Community of Scholars
- V-32 **GOODMAN, PAUL** / Growing Up Absurd
- V-932 **GRAUBARD, ALLEN** / Free the Children: Radical Reform and The Free School Movement
- V-457 **GREENE, FELIX** / The Enemy: Some Notes on the Nature of Contemporary Imperialism
- V-430 **GUEVERA, CHE** / Guerilla Warfare
- V-33 **HAMILTON, CHARLES AND STOKELY CARMICHAEL** / Black Power
- V-453 **HEALTH/PAC** / The American Health Empire
- V-635 **HEILBRONER, ROBERT L.** / Between Capitalism and Socialism
- V-283 **HENRY, JULES** / Culture Against Man
- V-482 **HETTER, PATRICIA AND LOUIS O. KELSO** / Two-Factor Theory: The Economics of Reality
- V-465 **HINTON, WILLIAM** / Fanshen: A Documentary of Revolution in a Chinese Village
- V-328 **HINTON, WILLIAM** / Iron Oxen
- V-2005 **HOARE, QUINTIN (ed.) AND KARL MARX** / Early Writings
- V-95 **HOFSTATDER, RICHARD** / The Age of Reform: From Bryan to FDR
- V-795 **HOFSTATDER, RICHARD** / America at 1750: A Social Portrait
- V-9 **HOFSTATDER, RICHARD** / The American Political Tradition
- V-686 **HOFSTATDER, RICHARD AND MICHAEL WALLACE (eds.)** / American Violence: A Documentary History
- V-317 **HOFSTATDER, RICHARD** / Anti-Intellectualism in American Life
- V-540 **HOFSTATDER, RICHARD AND CLARENCE L. VER STEEG (eds.)** / Great Issues in American History: From Settlement to Revolution, 1584-1776
- V-541 **HOFSTATDER, RICHARD (ed.)** / Great Issues in American History: From the Revolution to the Civil War, 1765-1865
- V-542 **HOFSTATDER, RICHARD (ed.)** / Great Issues in American History: From Reconstruction to the Present Day, 1864-1969
- V-385 **HOFSTATDER, RICHARD (ed.)** / The Paranoid Style in American Politics and Other Essays
- V-591 **HOFSTATDER, RICHARD (ed.)** / The Progressive Historians
- V-201 **HUGHES, H. STUART** / Consciousness and Society

| | |
|---|---|
| V-862 | **HUNNIUS, GERRY, DAVID G. GARSON AND JOHN CASE** / Workers Control: A Reader on Labor and Social Change |
| V-514 | **HUNTINGTON, SAMUEL F.** / The Soldier and the State |
| V-566 | **HURLEY, ROGER** / Poverty & Mental Retardation: A Causal Relationship |
| V-17 | **JAFFE, DENNIS AND TED CLARKE (eds.)** / Worlds Apart: Young People and The Drug Programs |
| V-241 | **JACOBS, JANE** / Death and Life of Great American Cities |
| V-584 | **JACOBS, JANE** / The Economy of Cities |
| V-433 | **JACOBS, PAUL** / Prelude to Riot |
| V-459 | **JACOBS, PAUL AND SAUL LANDAU WITH EVE PELL** / To Serve the Devil: Natives and Slaves Vol. I |
| V-460 | **JACOBS, PAUL AND SAUL LANDAU WITH EVE PELL** / To Serve the Devil: Colonials and Sojourners Vol. II |
| V-2017 | **JUDSON, HORACE FREELAND** / Heroin Addiction: What Americans Can Learn from the English Experience |
| V-790 | **KAPLAN, CAROL AND LAWRENCE (eds.)** / Revolutions, A Comparative Study |
| V-337 | **KAUFMANN, WALTER (trans.) AND FRIEDRICH NIETZSCHE** / Beyond Good and Evil |
| V-369 | **KAUFMANN, WALTER (trans.) AND FRIEDRICH NIETZSCHE** / The Birth of Tragedy and The Case of Wagner |
| V-985 | **KAUFMANN, WALTER (trans.) AND FRIEDRICH NIETZSCHE** / The Gay Science |
| V-401 | **KAUFMANN, WALTER (trans.) AND FRIEDRICH NIETZSCHE** / On the Genealogy of Morals and Ecce Homo |
| V-437 | **KAUFMANN, WALTER (trans.) AND FRIEDRICH NIETZSCHE** / The Will to Power |
| V-994 | **KELLNER, HANSFRIED AND PETER AND BRIGITTE BERGER** / The Homeless Mind: Modernization and Consciousness |
| V-482 | **KELSO, LOUIS O. AND PATRICIA HETTER** / Two-Factor Theory: The Economics of Reality |
| V-708 | **KESSLE, GUN AND JAN MYRDAL** / China: The Revolution Continued |
| V-510 | **KEY, V. O.** / Southern Politics |
| V-764 | **KLARE, MICHAEL T.** / War Without End: American Planning for the Next Vietnams |
| V-981 | **KLINE, MORRIS** / Why Johnny Can't Add: The Failure of the New Math |
| V-361 | **KOMAROVSKY, MIRRA** / Blue Collar Marriage |
| V-675 | **KOVEL, JOVEL** / White Racism |
| V-459 | **LANDAU, SAUL, PAUL JACOBS WITH EVE PELL** / To Serve the Devil: Natives and Slaves Vol. I |
| V-460 | **LANDAU, SAUL, PAUL JACOBS WITH EVE PELL** / To Serve the Devil: Colonials and Sojourners Vol. II |
| V-560 | **LASCH, CHRISTOPHER** / The Agony of the American Left |
| V-367 | **LASCH, CHRISTOPHER** / The New Radicalism in America |
| V-46 | **LASCH, CHRISTOPHER** / The World of Nations |
| V-987 | **LEKACHMANN, ROBERT** / Inflation: The Permanent Problem of Boom and Bust |
| V-880 | **LERNER, GERDA (ed.)** / Black Women in White America: A Documentary History |
| V-280 | **LEWIS, OSCAR** / The Children of Sanchez |

| | |
|---|---|
| V-634 | LEWIS, OSCAR / A Death in the Sanchez Family |
| V-421 | LEWIS, OSCAR / La Vida |
| V-370 | LEWIS, OSCAR / Pedro Martinez |
| V-533 | LOCKWOOD, LEE / Castro's Cuba, Cuba's Fidel |
| V-787 | MALDONADO-DENIS, DR. MANUEL / Puerto-Rico: A Socio-Historic Interpretation |
| V-406 | MARCUS, STEVEN / Engels, Manchester and The Working Class |
| V-480 | MARCUSE, HERBERT / Soviet Marxism |
| V-2002 | MARX, KARL AND DAVID FERNBACH (ed.) / Political Writings, Vol. I: The Revolutions of 1848 |
| V-2003 | MARX, KARL AND DAVID FERNBACH (ed.) / Political Writings, Vol. II: Surveys from Exile |
| V-2004 | MARX, KARL AND DAVID FERNBACH (ed). / Political Writings, Vol. III: The First International and After |
| V-2005 | MARX, KARL AND QUINTIN, HOARE (trans.) / Early Writings |
| V-2001 | MARX, KARL AND MARTIN NICOLOUS (trans.) / The Grundrisse: Foundations of the Critque of Political Economy |
| V-619 | McCONNELL, GRANT / Private Power and American Democracy |
| V-386 | McPHERSON, JAMES / The Negro's Civil War |
| V-928 | MEDVEDEV, ROY A. / Let History Judge: The Origins & Consequences of Stalinism |
| V-112 | MEDVEDEV, ZHORES A. / Ten Years After Ivan Denisovitch |
| V-427 | MENDELSON, MARY ADELAIDE / Tender Loving Greed |
| V-614 | MERMELSTEIN, DAVID (ed.) / The Economic Crisis Reader |
| V-307 | MIDDLETON, NIEL (ed.) AND I. F. STONE / The I. F. Stone's Weekly Reader |
| V-971 | MILTON, DAVID & NANCY AND FRANZ SCHURMAN (eds.) / The China Reader IV: People's China |
| V-905 | MITCHELL, JULIET / Woman's Estate |
| V-93 | MITFORD, JESSICA / Kind and Usual Punishment |
| V-539 | MORGAN, ROBIN (ed.) / Sisterhood is Powerful |
| V-389 | MOYNIHAN, DANIEL P. / Coping: On the Practice of Government |
| V-107 | MYRDAL, GUNNAR / Against the Stream: Critical Essays on Economics |
| V-730 | MYRDAL, GUNNAR / Asian Drama: An Inquiry into the Poverty of Nations |
| V-170 | MYRDAL, GUNNAR / The Challenge of World Poverty |
| V-793 | MYRDAL, JAN / Report from a Chinese Village |
| V-708 | MYRDAL, JAN AND GUN KESSLE / China: The Revolution Continued |
| V-834 | NEWTON, HUEY P. / To Die for the People |
| V-2001 | NICOLOUS, MARTIN (trans.) AND KARL MARX / The Grundrisse: Foundations of the Critique of Political Economy |
| V-377 | NIETZSCHE, FRIEDRICH AND WALTER KAUFMANN (trans.) / Beyond Good and Evil |
| V-369 | NIETZSCHE, FRIEDRICH AND WALTER KAUFMANN (trans.) / The Birth of Tragedy and The Case of Wagner |

| | |
|---|---|
| V-985 | **NIETZSCHE, FRIEDRICH AND WALTER KAUFMANN (trans.) /** The Gay Science |
| V-401 | **NIETZSCHE, FRIEDRICH AND WALTER KAUFMANN (trans.) /** On the Genealogy of Morals and Ecce Homo |
| V-437 | **NIETZSCHE, FRIEDRICH AND WALTER KAUFMANN (trans.) /** The Will to Power |
| V-803 | **NOVAK, ROBERT D. AND ROWLAND EVANS, JR. /** Nixon in the White House: The Frustration of Power |
| V-689 | **AN OBSERVER /** Message from Moscow |
| V-383 | **PIVEN, FRANCES FOX AND RICHARD CLOWARD /** The Politics of Turmoil: Essays on Poverty, Race & The Urban Crisis |
| V-743 | **PIVEN, FRANCES FOX AND RICHARD CLOWARD /** Regulating the Poor: The Functions of Public Welfare |
| V-128 | **PLATO /** The Republic |
| V-719 | **REED, JOHN /** Ten Days That Shook the World |
| V-791 | **REICH, WILHELM AND LEE BAXANDALL (ed.) /** Sex-Pol.: Essays 1929-1934 |
| V-159 | **REISCHAUER, EDWIN O. /** Toward the 21st Century: Education for a Changing World |
| V-622 | **ROAZEN, PAUL /** Freud: Political and Social Thought |
| V-204 | **ROTHSCHILD, EMMA /** Paradise Lost: The Decline of the Auto-Industrial Age |
| V-954 | **ROWBOTHAM, SHEILA /** Women, Resistance and Revolution |
| V-288 | **RUDOLPH, FREDERICK /** The American College and University |
| V-226 | **RYAN, WILLIAM /** Blaming the Victim |
| V-130 | **SALE, KIRKPATRICK /** Power Shift |
| V-965 | **SALE, KIRKPATRICK /** SDS |
| V-902 | **SALOMA, JOHN S. III AND FREDERICK H. SONTAG /** Parties: The Real Opportunity for Effective Citizen Politics |
| V-375 | **SCHELL, ORVILLE AND FRANZ SCHURMANN (eds.) /** The China Reader, Vol. I: Imperial China |
| V-376 | **SCHELL, ORVILLE AND FRANZ SCHURMANN (eds.) /** The China Reader, Vol. II: Republican China |
| V-377 | **SCHELL, ORVILLE AND FRANZ SCHURMANN (eds.) /** The China Reader. Vol. III: Communist China |
| V-738 | **SCHNEIR, MIRIAM (ed.) /** Feminism |
| V-375 | **SCHURMANN, FRANZ AND ORVILLE SCHELL (eds.) /** The China Reader, Vol. I: Imperial China |
| V-376 | **SCHURMANN, FRANZ AND ORVILLE SCHELL (eds.) /** The China Reader, Vol. II: Republican China |
| V-377 | **SCHURMANN, FRANZ AND ORVILLE SCHELL (eds.) /** The China Reader, Vol. III: Communist China |
| V-971 | **SCHURMANN, FRANZ AND NANCY AND DAVID MILTON (eds.) /** The China Reader, Vol. IV: People's China |
| V-89 | **SENNETT, RICHARD /** Families Against the City: Middle Class Homes of Industrial Chicago 1872-1890 |
| V-940 | **SENNETT, RICHARD AND JONATHAN COBB /** The Hidden Injuries of Class |
| V-308 | **SENNETT, RICHARD /** The Uses of Disorder |
| V-89 | **SENNETT, RICHARD /** Families Against the City: Middle Class Homes of Industrial Chicago, 1872-1890 |
| V-974 | **SERRIN, WILLIAM /** The Company and the Union |

| | |
|---|---|
| V-405 | **SERVICE, JOHN S. AND JOSEPH W. ESHERICK (ed.)** / Lost Chance in China: The World War II Despatches of John S. Service |
| V-798 | **SEXTON, BRENDAN AND PATRICIA** / Blue Collars and Hard Hats |
| V-279 | **SILBERMAN, CHARLES E.** / Crisis in Black and White |
| V-353 | **SILBERMAN, CHARLES E.** / Crisis in the Classroom |
| V-850 | **SILBERMAN, CHARLES E.** / The Open Classroom Reader |
| V-681 | **SNOW, EDGAR** / Red China Today: The Other Side of the River |
| V-930 | **SNOW, EDGAR** / The Long Revolution |
| V-902 | **SONTAG, FREDERICK H. AND JOHN S. SALOMA III** / Parties: The Real Opportunity for Effective Citizen Politics |
| V-388 | **STAMPP, KENNETH** / The Era of Reconstruction 1865-1877 |
| V-253 | **STAMPP, KENNETH** / The Peculiar Institution |
| V-959 | **STERN, PHILIP M.** / The Rape of the Taxpayer |
| V-547 | **STONE, I. F.** / The Haunted Fifties |
| V-307 | **STONE, I. F. AND NEIL MIDDLETON (ed.)** / The I. F. Stone's Weekly Reader |
| V-231 | **TANNENBAUM, FRANK** / Slave and Citizen: The Negro in the Americas |
| V-312 | **TANNENBAUM, FRANK** / Ten Keys to Latin America |
| V-984 | **THOMAS, PIRI** / Down These Mean Streets |
| V-322 | **THOMPSON, E. P.** / The Making of the Engish Working Class |
| V-810 | **TITMUSS, RICHARD** / The Gift Relationship: From Human Blood to Social Policy |
| V-848 | **TOFFLER, ALVIN** / The Culture Consumers |
| V-980 | **TOFFLER, ALVIN (ed.)** / Learning for Tomorrow: The Role of the Future in Education |
| V-731 | **TOLCHIN, MARTIN AND SUSAN** / To the Victor |
| V-686 | **WALLACE, MICHAEL AND RICHARD HOFSTATDER (eds.)** / American Violence: A Documentary History |
| V-957 | **WHALEN, CHARLES** / Your Right to Know |
| V-313 | **WILSON, EDMUND** / Apologies to the Iroquois |
| V-483 | **ZINN, HOWARD** / Disobedience and Democracy |